At the Threshold Of Memory

AT THE THRESHOLD OF MEMORY

A Bilingual Critical Anthology
of New and Selected Poems

MARJORIE AGOSÍN

Compiled & Edited by
Celeste Kostopulos-Cooperman

White Pine Press · Buffalo, New York

WHITE PINE PRESS
P.O. Box 236, Buffalo, New York 14201

Publication of this book was made possible, in part,
by Wellesley College,
the National Endowment for the Arts
and with public funds from the
New York State Council on the Arts, a State Agency.

Cover design: Elaine LaMattina

Cover painting: "Mujer que mira a los pajaros" by Ramon Levil.
Oil on cardboard. 38 X 56 cm. From the collection of Marjorie Agosín.

Printed and bound in the United States of America

First Edition

Library of Congress Control Number: 2003100356

*For my husband and lifelong partner, Gene,
and for my children, Adam and Sarah,
who understand and share
my passion for poetry and the Spanish language.*
–C.K.C.

MOTHERS AND CHILDREN

EXILE

THE DISPOSSESSED

TESTIMONIES

THE DEAD AND THE LIVING

THRESHOLDS OF DREAM AND DESIRE

ALCHEMIES OF THE HEART

THREADS OF HOPE

INTRODUCTION

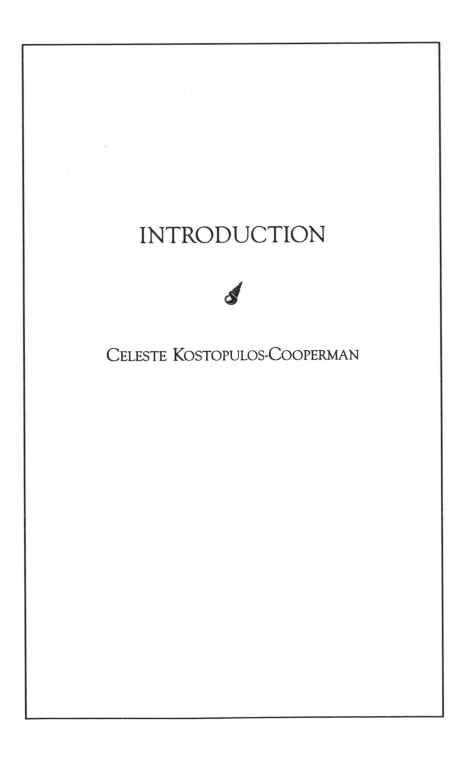

Celeste Kostopulos-Cooperman

An award-winning author of more than a dozen volumes of poetry and of numerous anthologies and essays of literary criticism, Marjorie Agosín knows how fundamental language is to an individual whose initiation into the world of literature began at the tender age of eight. Writing has always been an essential part of her life and a way to reflect upon her own experience as a writer in exile. It has also been the primary means through which Agosín has forged alliances with others that share her vision of a just and humane world.

Having been raised in a family of survivors of pogroms and holocausts, the Chilean writer's earliest recollections are filtered by the tempos and melodies of the rich mosaic of foreign idioms that surrounded her as a young girl. This confluence of languages, which at times created much confusion in the Agosín household, was to become a beacon in the young poet's life, guiding her through landscapes that had been preserved by her great-grandmothers, who could not detach themselves from the sounds, fragrances and images of the lands they had left behind. Marjorie Agosín observes, "The Babel of languages that was heard in my house, helped me reflect on the meaning of language and Diaspora. I saw how easily languages traveled from one country to another, opening new frontiers and closing others. But I also understood that the language of childhood was the most beautiful and intimate site of memory and affection."[1]

Although most of her books have been written on the North American continent, Marjorie Agosín continues to prefer Spanish for much of her creative work because this language belongs to a "sacred zone" that is connected to her early memories of life in the southern hemisphere. As she contemplates her writing life, she confesses that she never stopped writing in Spanish because she "could not abandon [her] essence, the fragile, divine core of [her] being. It would have meant becoming someone else, frequenting sadness, losing a soul and all the butterflies."[2] The reality of living in the United States and writing poetry and lyrical prose in Spanish necessitated having to live in translation and also be read in translation. By writing in Spanish, Agosín has been able to maintain her link to her homeland and ease the sorrow of early exile. She has also been able to share her life, her words, with those of us who have been privileged to translate her and make the beauty of her verse accessible to a wider reading public.

In her internationally acclaimed novel, *Fugitive Pieces*, the Toronto novelist Anne Michaels reflects on the nature of translation and suggests that, "You can choose your philosophy of translation just as you choose how to live....The poet moves from life to language, the translator moves from language to life. Both, like the immigrant, try to identify the invisible, what's between the lines, the mysterious implications."[3]

The movement from language to life can be likened to an exhilarating voyage that permits one access to other worlds filled with infinite possibilities. It is like crossing through a diaphanous threshold that erases the physical and temporal barriers between two otherwise detached worlds.

As the daughter of second-generation Greek immigrants I have always lived with two languages and cultures and have felt the strong emotional bonds that each has produced in my life. As a translator of Marjorie Agosín's poetry and lyrical narrative, I am constantly aware of the spaces between the lines and the mysterious, almost magical threads connecting these separate yet complementary pieces of our identities together. Ever since our first encounter on the campus of Wellesley College sixteen years ago, I have been deeply touched by Marjorie's luminous voice and her profound commitment to human rights. The daughter of second generation Jewish immigrants, Marjorie not only shares with other Latin American Jewish writers a tradition of multiple exiles and migrations, but also has experienced the sometimes irreconcilable conflicts that emerge between the mainstream culture of the New World and her Old World Eastern European heritage. As in the case of many of her Jewish Latin American contemporaries, the Spanish language has been a fundamental link connecting her Judaism to the much larger Hispanic tradition of the South American continent. As she herself reflects, "Being a Jewish writer in Latin America is also a way of connecting with the early experiences of Spanish Jews before the expulsion of 1492 and a way to continue the bond and carry the flourishing language of Sephardic heritage to diverse areas of the globe."[4]

A Chilean poet, who writes in Spanish and lives in an English-speaking country, Marjorie Agosín has been acutely aware of the need to be translated and understood by readers who do not share with her a common linguistic and cultural heritage. Describing her early years in the southern United States, she confesses that the experience of being translated had occurred in her daily life in that constant need to explain herself, to tell why her family was here, why they ate differently, why they had fled, why her accent was so thick, and why she did not look Hispanic.[5] As she began to be translated into English, the young poet felt that she no longer had to be explained or verified. She also felt that she was finally connected to a community of "invisible" readers who could experience the language of her childhood from the most remote places in the world.

This newly discovered sense of shared, personal experiences was to become a catalyst behind Marjorie Agosín's tireless efforts to tear down national and ethnic barriers and create a great "human community" of language. Her alliances with an international family of women writers would be accomplished through the numerous anthologies that she would publish alongside her creative ouevre—the most recent among these, *To Mend the World: Women Respond to 9/11* (2002) and *A Map of Hope: Women's Writing on Human Rights* (1999). In her own words, "This literature written by women conforms to my way of seeing, to my way of touching and to my experience as a reader. I empathize with their vision of the world. I also feel an almost ancestral connection to them that dates to my origins, to the first stories that I heard as a child from the voices of other women, grandmothers, mothers and maids."[6]

At its most basic level, a translation is but an aperture into another world, another culture, another way of seeing and feeling. It is an introduction that will carry some among us into uncharted places where new discoveries will be made and new perspectives experienced. As a cultural mediator, the translator must preserve as well as possible the substance and style of literary texts as they were originally intended so that they can continue to enrich the fabric of our lives. By collaborating with Marjorie Agosín on numerous projects throughout the years, I have at times felt like an archeologist, digging through layers of meaning and building bridges between the past and the present, the Old World and the New, so that readers of her work will experience the depth and beauty of her humanistic vision. Translating Marjorie's words has been very much a collaborative process: conversations and meetings at all times of day, revisions, phone calls, letters, postcards from distant lands, but most importantly, a partnership that has enriched and broadened our lives by also touching the intimate regions of our families and our shared experience of motherhood.

When Marjorie first suggested the idea of preparing a critical volume of this scope, I was very eager to begin the process. I was also, however, overwhelmed by the enormity of the assignment, for Marjorie Agosín is perhaps the most prolific writer of her generation. In both the South and North American continents she is recognized for the astonishing range of her work and for her indefatigable commitment to upholding the principles of social justice and human rights. Having been nurtured in a rich tradition of poetry, folktales and song, with María Luisa Bombal, Pablo Neruda, Gabriela Mistral and Nicanor Parra as her direct literary precursors, Marjorie Agosín has always felt very close to words and their melodies and to their remarkable power to heal and soothe. Literature has been a constant companion in the poet's life and it is through her extensive literary portfolio that Marjorie passionately demonstrates that writing is indeed an "act of faith, survival and transcendence."

Preparing a volume of selected poems is a daunting project because although on the surface it seems rather easy to arrange, trying to create an insightful guide to an individual's poetic vision presents several difficulties to the editor. Should one take the most direct route and proceed chronologically, volume by volume? Should specific themes be highlighted and poems selected according to the ways in which they reflect these themes? How might the volume most faithfully reveal the depth and evolution of the poet's artistic landscape?

According to Rolando Costa Picazo, the distinguished Argentine translator, the different languages that we speak condition our thoughts and our vision of life.[7] As a "codifier" of literary taste, the translator is ethically bound to respect as closely as possible the integrity of the source material by making the foreign familiar when there are apparently no immediate cultural analogs. The process of being translated, as Marjorie herself has observed, is truly an act of trust and human solidarity.

We are all enriched by translations. They are vital links that bond us to other people throughout the world and they are above all the primary means by which many readers, from the most erudite individuals to the most ordinary public, can learn about other ways of being and apprehending. As we journey through the pages of this volume, let us listen to the voices that inhabit the poet's thoughts and dreams. Let us also cross the threshold of her memory so that we can collaborate as readers in the recovery of lost and abandoned spaces and expand the realm of our own exuberant imaginations.

In this bilingual critical anthology the poems are arranged in sections which reflect themes and metaphors that are fundamental to Marjorie Agosin's artistic and critical *oeuvre*. Her rich Eastern European and Latin American heritage, her experience in exile, and her profound humanistic vision accompany the poet as she writes about her ancestors, about women and children, and about the poor and disinherited. Despite the often-difficult material that she examines, the poet also expresses a need to rejoice in life, to hope and believe in the possibility of change. Indeed, much of Agosin's writing can be characterized as a celebration of life and a refusal to yield to the brutal realities and chaos that surface in the worlds she describes.[8] Her love of homeland and her encounter with her own ancestral language have also made memory and the obligation to recover and preserve the past an essential part of her writing life.

Through her numerous volumes of poetry and lyrical prose, Marjorie Agosin, essayist, professor, storyteller and human rights activist, attempts to retrieve familiar spaces. She also attempts to share the private zones of her own memory and experience with the collective memory of others that have made exile and the Jewish and Latin American Diasporas a way of life. Her poetry draws her closer to the universal community of individuals who intuit and feel the tremendous power of words. She writes verses that are nurtured and inspired with hope and images that remind us all of the underlying beauty and goodness of a world threatened continuously by fear, hatred, political oppression, and violence.

The granddaughter of Russian and Viennese Jewish exiles, Agosín spent most of her childhood in Santiago, Chile and grew up in the old neighborhood of Nuñoa where she would wonder often about the lives of beggar women in the streets with their hand-me-down skirts and tattered black shawls. As a young girl she also loved the companionship of the household servants who arrived with broken suitcases to dwell in backrooms surrounded by photographs of borrowed children. These women, who had renounced permanence and devoted their lives to caring for her and her family, taught her at a very innocent age about the meaning of true happiness. Through her *nanas* she discovered the simple joys found in the melodies of birds singing delicate tunes or in the aromas of fresh baked bread and boldo leaves filtering through the house.

At the Hebrew Institute on Macul Street, Marjorie Agosín received a broad, liberal education and learned to speak and write in both Spanish and Hebrew. In Marta Alvarado's history class she also learned about justice and the benefits of collective socialism. Through the charitable acts of her maternal grandfather, José Halpern, who had helped many refugees fleeing the Nazi menace during the war years, 1938-1943, Agosín also was raised in a household where the seeds of her political activism were cultivated.

Her Jewish education gave her an identity and above all a respect for human life. A witness to her mother Frida's generosity toward the refugee women who passed through her house year after year smelling of poverty and foreign places, and the selfless example of her father, Moisés Agosín, who gave up practicing medicine because he didn't have the heart to charge his patients, also exposed her to an altruism that would have a profound influence on her life-long commitment to defending the rights of others much less fortunate than she. If political action, denunciation and apprenticeship were the "sacred ingredients" of her childhood, then poetry and writing were to become the "sacred tools" of her survival and hope. Hearing stories about losses and absences and experiencing first-hand the alienation of racial prejudice and exile, both in Chile and later in the United States, Marjorie Agosín learned at an early age that "oppression and pain go much further than the color of one's skin."[9] As a young Jewish girl growing up in a predominantly Catholic country, she felt a strong connection to her ancestral past and an obligation to preserve and honor the memories of those who were left behind.

Marjorie Agosín belongs to a generation of writers and artists who have dedicated much of their writing lives to defending human rights and educating an international public about the plight of the "disappeared" and other politically oppressed groups in the world. As a feminist and descendant of Jews who fled the pogroms of Czarist Russia and the extermination camps of a demented Europe, Marjorie also has felt a particular obligation to speak on behalf of women and other marginalized minorities who have resisted cruelty and injustice wherever they have surfaced. Unlike some of her Jewish Latin American contemporaries, however, Agosín does not see the Jewish female as a marginal being within the confines of her own cultural heritage. On the contrary, the traditions and the link recovered by memory empower her women and give them a voice and identity in a land that can no longer remain indifferent to their lives.

Similar to the Mexican, Margot Glantz, and the Argentine, Alicia Steimberg, in much of Marjorie Agosín's writings we find an almost irresistible longing to remember and reconstruct the history of the family. Through her memoirs, *A Cross and a Star* (1995), *Always from Somewhere Else* (1998), and *The Alphabet in My Hands: A Writing Life* (2000) she explores the coffers of memory and creates a mosaic of vivid and often discontinuous images and stories that are fragments of a past, present and future to which she belongs. Likewise in the recently published *The Angel of Memory* (2002), the poet continues to piece together her own identity by revisiting the distant and fading world of her German-speaking Omamá Helena, whose eyes contained the sadness of unspeakable loss and grief. As Marjorie and her mother return to Vienna half a century after the war, they both realize that memory is not so much nostalgia for the past, but something very alive and timeless. In "El gólem de Praga," the poet writes: "Sé que vivimos en la memoria, o en la metáfora de la memoria, o en la memoria que no deja olvidos, que no permite promesas, o en la imaginación de una memoria que juega con la distancia ... / I know we live in memory, or in the metaphor of memory, or in memory that does not allow oblivion or in the imagination of a memory that plays with distance...." As an angel of memory, a winged messenger of God, a guardian of sacred, luminous family truths that must be recovered and preserved for future generations, the great-grandmother becomes a vital connection to a past that informs and shapes the great-granddaughter's present. Writing for Marjorie Agosín and other Jewish Latin Americans becomes a process that often leads to self-discovery and in some cases, survival. The poet confesses, "Words gave me back my imagination. Words were fireflies, threads of transgression, of faith. Writing was not a hopeless return to the realm of enchantment or the silence of magic and mist that uncovers the light, but above all else the most intense pleasure, the brightest of all lights. Writing saved my life."[10] It is through language that these authors redefine their own identities and come to terms with their personal legacies. In his essay, "Jewish Writers and Collective Memory," Leonardo Senkman speculates that the autobiographical literature being written by Jewish men and women is the result of the deconstruction of national identity. He especially cites the Southern Cone nations of Argentina, Chile and Uruguay that experienced the trauma of political exile and violence in the recent past. "For these writers, calling forth memory has become a way to mark the disenchantment that has uprooted them as citizens, but which simultaneously permitted them, as writers, to also be Jews."[11]

Marjorie Agosín's Jewish heritage and human rights activism in and beyond Chile coincided with her passion for always forming alliances with marginal beings and victims of political oppression. She sensed herself as one of them. "The experience of not having been one of *them*, of not having disappeared, had an immense impact on my conception of the world. I was a survivor who must not succumb to an accomplice silence... Not doing anything was as good as being guilty. It was like being part of that amalgam of ordinary people who perform evil acts."[12]

In *Brujas y algo más / Witches and Other Things* (1984), a seminal volume which anticipates much of her future writing and human rights activism, Marjorie Agosín invokes the memory of the disappeared and swears to keep them alive through her words, "Yo juro ser la palabra/ pero nunca lamentar a los/ muertos que hoy y siempre/ están." ("I swear to be the word/ but never to lament/ the dead who are present/ Now. Forever.")

The shadows of the disappeared that will haunt the poet in later years and come to dominate her verse, begin to accompany her in these early poems. In *Brujas y algo más*, Marjorie Agosín emerges as a fresh, unpretentious and sometimes irreverent voice. Her verses range from the very personal to the testimonial. Unwilling to accept restrictions marked conventionally by gender, she writes with defiant candor and challenges the traditional phallocentric culture of her time. Beyond the universal themes of love, death, identity and friendship, she also writes about exile and questions the humanity of those who deny the dignity of the individual. Agosín is a poet passionately committed to the truth, as unsettling as it may be. Her verse both consoles and celebrates the beauty that some try to erase.

In 1972, Marjorie Agosín's family moved to Athens, Georgia where her father had accepted an appointment as a professor of chemistry at the university. As circumstances would have it, the decision to remain in the United States occurred shortly after the military coup that overthrew the democratically-elected government of Salvador Allende. This was to be a dramatic turning point in the young poet's life because she felt more and more as an outsider in the small community that had already defined her as a young Jewish girl with a Spanish accent. Fulfilling the eternal tradition of her ancestors, the first years after her arrival in the U.S. her family lived the life of poor immigrants, in empty houses with loaned furniture. In her own words: "Judaism and the diasporic condition of my family became an emblematic metaphor for lost and irrecoverable things."[13] This experience of vulnerability and "otherness," as difficult as it was for a fifteen year old girl, seemed to raise her conscience even further and compel her to identify with the fate of the disappeared women who populated her nightmares in the dark silence of the stone house in Georgia. In her personal memoir she writes, "I was safe in a house made of stone surrounded by enormous pine trees. Yet my destiny joined theirs. Perhaps I had also disappeared. No one could pronounce my last name without breaking into laughter, no one knew who I was. I found myself unable to feel at home in that lost territory where I had been set ashore and abandoned."[14]

In later years Marjorie Agosín came to believe that exile and memory and the ability to see her country from the periphery heightened her sensitivity toward the situation of women and the state of human rights in Chile and Latin America in particular.[15] In *Mujeres de humo (Women of Smoke)* (1988), she dedicates an entire volume to many types of women: old, haggard, senile, young, poor, beautiful, abandoned, desperate, strong, weak, lonely and imaginative beings fundamentally joined by their gender and sense of powerlessness. Like the smoke that surrounds them, they rise from the embers and demand visibility. Through her poetic sensibility, Marjorie Agosín shows us how the ancient mythological stereotypes of women have perpetuated unacceptable images that must be discarded and replaced with more honest and realistic ones. Even the suicide, "oyéndose en nuestra ausencia" ("echoing in our absence"), clamors for recognition amid the stones of a vast and vaporous shore.

As a "guardian of memory" Marjorie Agosín writes to recover what was once lost and to preserve the past from the silence of forgetting. In her poem "Recordar" from *Hogueras / Bonfires* (1990), the act of remembering is a sacred ritual that originates in the depths of a soul unwilling to let oblivion erase the images of another time. These images linger in Agosín's poetic conscience and continue to prey on her mind even when the subject matter appears far removed from the not-too-distant past. "Salem," a poem that evokes unsettling images of the seventeenth century New England witch trials, foreshadows the Holocaust imagery of her later poetry and prose. The lasting image that we have, however, is not that of a woman made of smoke, dancing crippled through the bonfires, but of a woman transformed by her inner beauty and goodness into an unfurled fan spreading its fragrance of stars and roses throughout the earth.

Much of Marjorie Agosín's poetry and lyrical prose is inspired by the courage and tenacity of women who have suffered unimaginable hardships and in many cases death, in periods of political upheaval. In the prologue to her book, *Zonas de dolor / Zones of Pain* (1988), Agosín tells her readers how the poems kept growing in her dreams until she found the language that would draw her closer to her dead sisters and help keep their memory alive in the hearts and minds of others. "Me vigilaban, a veces me despertaban acariciándome, más que nada me pedían que no las olvide." ("They watched over me, sometimes they woke me up caressing me, above all they asked me not to forget them.")[16]

This same imperative to not be *forgotten* is echoed further still in the poem, "Ana Frank y nosotras," where Anne Frank and other dead women approach and gaze at the poet imploring her to survive them, tell them and be them. In yet another poem a disappeared woman clamors to come back from the labyrinths, to return and name herself before the silence of oblivion. And in "Los ojos de los enterrados," the penetrating gaze and restlessness of the disappeared disturb the poet's thoughts and beseech her to remember them. The poet's words become bridges connecting the living with the dead, the dead with the living.

In *Zones of Pain*, Agosín in her quest for social justice and respect for human rights explores the madness of a society in which freedom has been replaced by terror and lawlessness. By identifying with the victims themselves, she penetrates a very private world of physical and emotional pain. A dark, desolate region that few would enter willingly, the poet is compelled to articulate the disturbing human dramas that resulted from the oppressive and violent political machinery of Augusto Pinochet that devastated her nation. She also questions the morality and ethics of a complicitous society whose silence conceals truths that need to be spoken. In "Lo más increíble" she specifically confronts the dilemma of the survivors who must come to terms with the knowledge that the executioners are still among them, occupying the spaces of ordinary citizens and believing in the righteousness of their actions. As unbelievable as it may seem, assassins walk the streets with impunity, and a nation that continues to harbor these criminals dares to call itself civilized. "Y lo más increíble/era gente/como usted/como yo/sí, gente fina/como nosotros." ("And the most unbelievable part/they were people/like you/like me/yes, nice people/just like us.") Her language is simple and direct and her tone reserved, yet the words of the poet speak with a sincerity that is all too real to ignore.

In the two year interval between her next book of poems and her immersion in human rights themes and learning how to write about and describe the pain of the tortured body, Marjorie Agosín turned to the sumptuous beauty of the natural world, perhaps in an effort to preserve life in the midst of overwhelming chaos and grief. In *Hogueras / Bonfires*, a woman's voice predominates and expresses her most intimate feelings and hopes. The tone is often self-reflective and assured and the desire is to be like "las cosas que alumbran," "things that radiate light." Sometimes simple objects trigger sensuous, erotic desire, as in the poem, "Castañas en el aire," where the stimulus is a golden mouth-watering chestnut. Likewise in "Invierno en la Plaza de Mayo," Agosín eroticizes a political space. The images of birds singing and eating corn from the hands of the poet and of lovers imagining a common future displace the sadness and grief that most associate with this spot.

Despite her attempts, conscious or otherwise, to keep the brutality and the excesses of the dictatorial regimes at bay, Marjorie Agosín cannot hush the disquieting voices that compel her to write and speak for those who did not survive the years of military oppression. In the poem "Cordilleras," death and solitude erupt in language consumed by a woman's loss and abandonment. The "hogueras" that burn in this provocative and sensorial volume burst with the passion of erotic pleasure and at times explode with a rage that seeks expression through verse.

This is groundbreaking poetry within a Latina feminist context. As others have revealed, "Agosín writes with a lyrical style free of moral restraint and inhibition toward the female body ... [She] reworks the traditional poetic discourse of men in such a way that the woman is in control."[17] According to the poet, "*Bonfires* is a very sensuous, very erotic book, in which the object of desire is the body, itself... [it is] a celebration of the material aspect of the body, of the dynamics of the couple, of the smells, the spaces, the things that vibrate with life, of the water that flows through the body, of the soul, of the movement of bodies that dream."[18]

Indeed, it is through her own self-actualization that the female poetic voice is empowered to chronicle her eroticism in a lyrical discourse that rises from the depths of her being. Through her memory and words, the poet recreates the passion embraced and felt within the intimate thresholds of desire.

Marjorie Agosín's delight in the sensuous pleasures of the body reflects a deeply humanistic vision that transcends the horror and anguish that often emerge from the political realities that she portrays. In books like *Travesías generosas / Generous Journeys* (1992) and *Sargazo / Sargasso* (1993), the poet continues to celebrate life by turning her creative sensibility toward the sumptuous vegetation and landscape of her homeland. For Agosín, "All of America is sensual, from the exuberant mountains to the leafy jungles, to the restless seas...these are poems to be recited aloud, to be sung, to be danced and eaten."[19] In *Generous Journeys* Marjorie Agosín chooses as her subject matter plants, spices and fruits of the Americas. Like her noble predecessor Pablo Neruda, she sings in praise of foods that permeate the landscape of the New World. She also draws us closer to the people who cultivate and harvest them. "Azúcar" is a poem that celebrates the sweetness and beauty of sugar cane, which is also an emblematic plant associated with invasion, social injustice and oppression. The poet's social conscience permeates her verse as she meditates on the colonization of Cuba and its plantation economy of the past. The *mate* in "Yerba mate" is also a palliative that accompanies and soothes the souls of those who drink it. "A sacred hospitable friend/ a constant companion/ sunny, always lively/ true guardian/ mossy jewel... Like the *azúcar*, it shares a mysterious, secretive link with the sadness of those who taste it. Whether she is extolling the delicate, fragrant mouth-watering qualities of the wild strawberry or the healing powers of the chile pepper which is as diverse as the people whose pallets it adorns, through these ode-like poems Agosín spiritually reconnects with her homeland, invoking the aromas, flavors and textures that pervaded the country of her youth.

In *Sargasso*, similarly, we encounter poetry that is deeply rooted in the poet's humanity and love of the natural world. The *sargasso* grass swaying on the windy shore possesses its own rhythms, sounds and language, and water images are closely linked to memories of a past filled with voyages on the sea and a yearning for a better life. In the poem "Tocando el cielo," the poet celebrates the possibilities of life when she is at the shore. To touch the water, which is the sky, is to know that happiness and tranquillity are within reach. Water assuages the sorrow of the exile and comforts the poet in her solitude. In this beautiful poetry, Marjorie Agosín does not submit to despair. She insists instead on the power of the individual to search for and find a life of hope and peace.

Since it is in a mother's love where we often encounter the most selfless examples of tenacity and courage amid hopelessness and loss, Agosín has dedicated a significant portion of her critical and artistic work to them. Her documentary volumes about the Chilean *arpilleristas* and the Mothers of the Plaza de Mayo venerate women who through their love and extraordinary valor have raised the conscience of the world in an effort to create a more just and decent society. In *Zones of Pain*, as a prelude to *Circles of Madness: Mothers of the Plaza de Mayo (1992)*, the Chilean poet writes a memorial to the women of the Plaza de Mayo. This is a haunting poem that rises above the shapes and beyond the echoes of women praying, questioning and screaming with rage as they search for the truth that lies buried within the pain of indifference that surrounds them.

In *Circles of Madness* the poet does not fear the dead. She talks to them and wants to promise them that they did not die in vain and that as long as she is able, she will keep their memory alive. *Circles* is dedicated to the brave Argentine women whose sons and daughters disappeared under the military dictatorship of Jorge Videla which began in 1976 and lasted until 1983 when Raúl Alfonsín rose to the presidency. As in *Zones*, Marjorie Agosín crosses the threshold between the dead and the living to communicate with the tortured-disappeared and to reduce the pain left by their absence. In the poem "¿Cuántas veces yo converso con mis muertos?" Agosín is haunted by the dead/disappeared whose "faces are a memory of sorrows." She also once again explores the moral and ethical question of collective responsibility and emphasizes her belief that human rights, when they are violated, become the concerns of humanity as a whole. "Mis muertos que a lo mejor son tuyos" reflects this deep-seated conviction.

Human rights and political oppression are fundamental and recurrent themes in Marjorie Agosín's writings. In her preface to An *Absence of Shadows* (1998), a volume that is dedicated to Reneé Eppelbaum, founding member of the Mothers of the Plaza de Mayo, Agosín declares that "One is born with human rights, and thus one is sacredly connected to all living things. When human rights are violated, so is the sacredness of our world. Neighbors who rape and murder neighbors and civil authorities who torture the children of friends are among the darkest shadows on our century. Civilians have become tyrants in what was once the province of the military, and in these wars there can never be victory, only ashes and a sea of tears."[20]

The poems in *Circles of Madness* are about absence, grief and loneliness—a solitude that is forced upon the individual who must live with the memories, the shadows of those who once were. As in *Women of Smoke* and *Bonfires*, smoke is a recurring image, "país de humo." Its presence obscures, like the darkness, and distorts as well as erases. However, behind the unsettling images and deep within the volume, is a profound desire to resurrect the dead and turn their lives into a song of love that will transcend generations and exist for all eternity. A beautiful homage to the extraordinary strength of those women who dared defy the brutality of a fascist military dictatorship that denied human dignity and mutilated an entire generation of people, *Circles of Madness* venerates the remarkable courage of women who tirelessly sustain the hope that is needed to demand accountability and find light where there is darkness.

Growing up among exiles and among loved ones who had suffered unimaginable losses in the Holocaust has made Marjorie Agosín feel a very intimate and personal bond to others living on the margin. There is a strong link between the poet's Jewish heritage and identity and her devotion to victims of political oppression and violence. Although all the memories are not personally hers, as Laura Riesco so poignantly observes, there is in Agosín's poetry, fiction and essays an "insistence upon never forgetting or ignoring the pain that bigotry and oppression caused her sisters, her fellow Jews, and all those punished by repressive regimes...."[21]

Through her poetry and lyrically-inspired prose, Marjorie Agosín approaches what she herself defines as "the essence, the inner voice of poetry: a dialogue with memory, a meditation against forgetting." In her prologue to *Dear Anne Frank*, (1994), Agosín reflects on how memory "has an indelible way" of selecting what from the past is timeless and sacred. She also describes how her great-grandmother Helena would revive the memory of her loved ones by kissing their photos every night before going to bed, thus preventing their stories from falling into oblivion.

Through the photograph of Anne Frank that her grandfather had given her in the summer of 1970, two years before she was to depart for the United States, Agosín tries to duplicate her great-grandmother's ritual and preserve through her verse the life of this young Jewish girl who perished in a concentration camp months before the liberation. She says that her dialogue with Anne began with a paradoxical desire to remember and to forget—to preserve Anne's humanity but to forget her as a martyr. Marjorie Agosín's curiosity and compassion allow her to imagine what the life of this thirteen-year-old girl was like in the darkness of the secret annex where she was forced to live. She is consumed with an obsessive desire to revive her in the hearts and minds of all who strive to protect the human race from horrors similar to those of the Nazi menace.

In her lyrical dialogue with Anne Frank, Agosín raises serious questions that not only "rethink" the moral character of citizens who submitted to the Nazis but also of those who silently and passively watched as the military dictatorships of Latin America destroyed thousands of lives. In this volume, the Chilean poet makes a clear connection between all victims of genocide and tries to find a way to help survivors memorialize the lives of their loved ones, "people who are without graves," and whose "bodies eternally sleep somewhere in the air."

The not-too-distant experience of her own country and the harsh consequences suffered under military rule for more than a decade are compelling reasons for the poet to examine the contemptible legacy of racism and the human tragedy of nationalism. As a poet, Marjorie Agosín knows how deeply rooted words are to the soul, and as a Jewish Latin American writer, she also knows that language is a medium through which the past must be remembered and honored. *Dear Anne Frank* is a powerful collection of poems that speak with compassion and love and give voice to the departed and to those who are not able to speak for themselves.

The imagination of our Chilean poet is like a paintbrush that evokes vivid and sometimes haunting images of the places and the people that she writes about. In the poem "Puentes"/"Bridges," which appears in the volume *Hacia la ciudad espléndida / Toward the Splendid City* (1994), Agosín describes "poetry's boundary" as a place where "words are not borders but rather gestures, /strange, seagoing letters for lost and wise sailors." Her poetry is a "bridge" that connects her to the world and people around her. Her lyrics allow her to transcend physical boundaries and navigate landscapes nurtured by her humanity and ability to continue to feel a sense of awe before life's wonder, "el asombro de la vida," despite the relentless signs of misery and cruelty that remain.

As we have seen countless times before, Agosín however, is not a poet of despair. She clings tenaciously to hope and defiantly confesses her alliance with the powerless and abandoned citizens of the world. In "Lo que era Yugoslavia"/"What was Yugoslavia," invisible corpses of dead angel-children inhabit the landscape of a country which has been devastated by the violence and bloodshed of war. Still, in spite of the human suffering, the poet assures us that there are those who maintain the ability to feel life's wonder, "la posibilidad del asombro."

In *Toward the Splendid City*, Marjorie Agosín continues to examine subjects that occupy the core of human existence and endurance. Through her sometimes haunting yet lyrical descriptions of urban landscapes and their inhabitants, the poet reveals the horrors of human suffering and the importance of compassion and love in a world that can no longer afford to remain indifferent to the plight of others. All the poems in this collection speak to us with a humanity that beckons to be heard and that towers above the cruelty and the devastation that preceded it. In this volume Agosín's poetic vision reaches beyond the familiar landscapes of her youth and encompasses regions of the world where darkness and human tragedy have left their indelible insignias. Whether she is writing about Chile, Argentina, or cities in Central America, Eastern Europe or the Middle East, Marjorie Agosín through the power of her lyrics, touches a sympathetic chord in all who dare journey with her and examine the underlying core of human existence in all its beauty and splendor.

Far removed from the disquieting images of political oppression, cruelty and fear, Agosín chooses as the subject matter of her next volume of poetry the beautiful landscape of southern France where she imagines herself as the Dutch artist, Vincent Van Gogh. In this poetry of sensuous beauty, colors stream from the poet's impressionist brush strokes with incandescent light revealing eternal sunflowers and fields of lavender that "shun the night in its prophecy of shadows."

Winner of the Letras de Oro Prize, *Noche Estrellada/Starry Night* (1996) is a collection of bewitching poetry where identities are blurred and the surrounding landscape becomes a source of inspiration and wonder before bare life itself, in all its clarity and vastness. As the poetic voice confesses in "The Alchemy of the Palate," "I like to draw close/ to the earth's beginning...to trace the orifice,/ probe the earth as if it were/ the mouth of love."

This is passionate poetry where the beauty of the naked body is wrapped in a blanket of sweet air and sunlight and painting becomes a desperate expression of survival and love. "Yo he venido a pintar/que es como amar/ que es como estar despierto/ en el centro de la noche/ que es como la luz y palpitar." ("I have come to paint, which is like loving, which is like being awake in the middle of the night, which is like yearning and trembling for light.")

Agosín is clearly a poet who loves to rejoice in life. In *Starry Night* the landscape, although foreign, is familiar and the beauty, love, passion and madness that exist within the verses are themes that radiate with a desire to experience life in all its fullness, to recognize "the flow of the forest" and the "colors which are the fragrances of happiness."

In her most recent poetry, Marjorie Agosín turns her gaze once again upon women who have inspired her through their strength, courage and love. *Mujeres melodiosas/Melodious Women* (1997) is like an album containing the portraits of individuals who dared to live and be who they were. In this collection Agosín reflects upon the lives of ordinary and extraordinary women, of poets, writers, aristocrats, peasants, activists, mothers, daughters, wives and widows who, as different as they all are, embrace a common bond of shared humanity, determination and daring to live and die with all their restless yearnings.

As in earlier poems, Agosín continues to capture the alternating rhythms, landscapes and infinite beauty of the natural world. Where others see only darkness and despair, she sees fireflies and golden seeds, willow trees, green rivers, unbelievable fragrances and islands "where life is a golden corner of orange blossoms and unspoken times." Through her soothing lyrics she is able to walk calmly among the shadows, make alliances with the dead and in "Titania's Creed," dream about a world where "there would be no borders, only the eyes of the just."

Like the "Hacedora de palabras"/"Maker of Words," who seems to emerge from the elements themselves and who breathes life into words that begin as extensions of her own being, Marjorie Agosín's poetry, indeed much of her writing, is a meditation on humanity and a deliberate attempt to preserve the past and all that she had left behind. "Poetry has saved me from oblivion, from forgetting, and from walking the earth as a stranger."[22]

Her poems both old and new also reflect a desire to penetrate the darkness and confront the evil that continues to violate and destroy the lives of so many innocent victims. In *El consejo de las hadas/Council of the Fairies* (1997), Marjorie Agosín's main protagonists are women and children who have suffered extreme hardship because of war, political injustice and human rights abuses. As in previous books, Agosín's humane vision is one that is compelled to address the presence of evil wherever it may surface. There is always, however, a sense that change is possible and that hope and beauty can be found in the hearts and minds of those who dare to defy the inhumane actions of the few.

The greatest weapon against injustice and repression is the refusal to accept the presence of cruelty and oppression wherever is exists, and the commitment to eradicate it whenever it appears. Coming from a situation of privilege does not free an individual from the obligation, albeit the responsibility to denounce the assassins of truth and goodness, nor does it make it impossible to empathize with the plight of those who are less fortunate. It also does not give a select few the right to shape and determine the fate of others.

In an interview that appeared in *Lilith* (summer 1990), Marjorie Agosín reflects on the concept of social privilege and says that "[We] must work through *circular understanding,* that is, we must come to know that the Mapuche Indian woman has much to teach us, that women of the Third World know more than we do about what it means to be human, to be kind."[23] Perhaps this is why Agosín writes so often about peasants and beggar women and in the poem "Muñeca de trapo"/"Rag Doll," advises her daughter to be Pancha's guardian, to cover her and never mistake the privilege of [her] silk sheets. "Quiero que seas la guardiana de la Pancha/ que la cubras/y que no confundas/ jamás el privilegio/ de tus sábanas de seda."

There is much joy and beauty in Marjorie Agosín's poetry of witness and truth. The Chilean poet chooses life over destruction and celebrates and rejoices in the bounty and love that surround her. In the desert landscapes that appear in *Lluvia en el desierto/Rain in the Desert* (1999), Agosín continues to explore themes that touch the human soul and remind us that we are all travelers in a universe that awaits our sensibilities and "human touch." Like her ancestors, she, too, is drawn to the desert, which illuminates everyone and everything that wanders through its sands.

Always searching for life's bare essentials, often in a sparse language that reflects a fundamental need to reveal the common threads that unite all humanity, Marjorie Agosín explores diverse landscapes: the sea, the desert, cities, prison cells, and the human body to "make beauty and order out of pain and chaos." Her journey, however, is not always motivated from anguish, but rather from a refusal to yield to despair and a desire to search for the light, i.e., the hope, that others often do not see. As she so beautifully pronounces in "El tiempo claro del amor," (Love's Clear Time) "Todo era claro, clarividente./ Nada oscuro había en el fondo de las cosas./ Tanta luz había en mis espaldas./ Negué la oscuridad cóncava de las ciudades, la avaricia." "Everything was clear, clairvoyant./ Nothing was obscure in the depth of things./ There was so much light on my back./ I denied the concave darkness of cities, the greed." At the threshold of memory, the poet's words nourish the earth with cascading dreams of peace that deny the darkness like a desert rain sustaining life in all its sublime wonder.

Notes to the Introduction

[1] Marjorie Agosín, "A Dream of Babel," *I Carry My Roots With Me / Touchpoints of the Latin American Jewish Diaspora* (The District of Columbia Jewish Community Center, 2000), p. 29.

[2] Marjorie Agosín, *The Alphabet in My Hands: A Writing Life* (New Jersey: Rutgers University Press, 2000), p. 144.

[3] Anne Michaels, *Fugitive Pieces* (New York: Vintage Books, 1998), p. 109.

[4] Marjorie Agosín, "A Dream of Babel," p. 31.

[5] Marjorie Agosín, "Always Living in Spanish," *Multicultural Review*, 1999.

[6] Marjorie Agosín, "A Necklace of Words," *Multicultural Review*, 2000.

[7] "The Art of Rolando Costa Picazo,"an unpublished essay by Paula Durbin.

[8] Barbara Mujica, "Marjorie Agosín Weaves Magic with a Social Vision," in *Américas*, Vol. 45, No. 1 (January, 1993), p. 47.

[9] Marjorie Agosín, "Through a Field of Stars I Remember," in *King David's Harp: Autobiographical Essays by Jewish-American Writers*, edited by Stephen Sadow (University of New Mexico Press, 1999), pp. 187-200.

[10] Marjorie Agosín, *The Alphabet in My Hands: A Writing Life*, p. 146.

[11] Leonardo Senkman, "Jewish Writers and Collective Memory," in *Tradition and Innovation: Reflections on Latin American Jewish Writing*, edited by Robert DiAntonio and Nora Glickman (New York: State University of New York Press, 1993), p. 34.

[12] Agosín, "Through a Field of Stars," p. 196.

[13] Agosín, "Through a Field of Stars," p.196.

[14] Agosín, *The Alphabet in My Hands*, p. 103.

[15] B. Mujica, "Marjorie Agosín Weaves Magic with Social Vision," p. 46.

[16] Marjorie Agosín in prologue to *Zones of Pain* (New York: White Pine Press, 1988).

[17] Juan Villegas, "Introduction: Agosín: The Road to Transgression" (Arizona: Bilingual Press, 1990).

[18] Mujica interview, p. 47.

[19] Mujica, p. 48.

[20] Marjorie Agosín, Preface to *An Absence of Shadows* (New York: White Pine Press, 1998), p.11.

[21] Laura Riesco, Forward to *A Cross and a Star: Memoirs of a Jewish Girl in Chile* (New York: The Feminist Press, 1997), p. xiv.

[22] Agosín, Preface to *An Absence of Shadows*, p. 12.

[23] "Marjorie Agosín: A Woman, a Jew and a Chilean." Interview in *Lilith: A Magazine for Jewish Women*, summer 1990, p. 12.

EDITOR'S NOTE

I have been privileged to work with Dennis Maloney and Elaine LaMattina of White Pine Press, who have supported my work as a translator of creative prose and poetry for more than a decade. Having collaborated with Marjorie Agosín on a substantial body of work, they provided me with invaluable editorial assistance in the design of this bilingual edition of new and selected poems by the critically acclaimed poet. It is particularly gratifying for me to work with individuals so committed to enriching our literary heritage by supporting authors whose voices cross cultural, ethnic and geographic boundaries.

The publication of this book coincides with the 30th anniversary of White Pine Press which has throughout the years brought the humanistic vision of Marjorie Agosín to the English-reading public. I cannot think of a better way to honor the lives of people who are so dedicated to promoting the belief that literature is a means through which the peoples of this ever-changing world can achieve a heightened understanding and respect toward one another.

—Celeste Kostopulos-Cooperman
Suffolk University
Boston, Massachusetts

At night,
only your steps,
sacred memory,
other times.

en la noche,
tan sólo tus pasos,
sagrada memoria
de otros tiempos.

The Angel of Memory
                    L.N.

GENEALOGIES

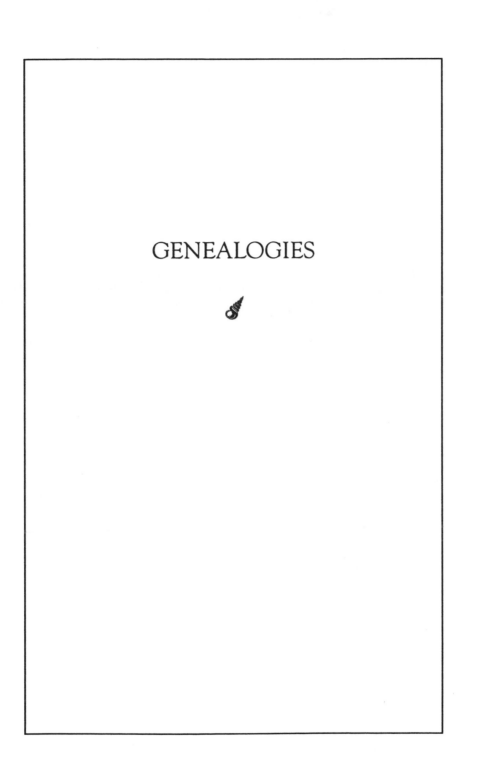

MI ABUELA

Mi abuela
la esplendorosa
Josefina
la que cruzó la
cordillera
de los Andes
a pie y en mula,
la que amó
los ojos verdes
del finado Allende,
la que tiene 84 años
y a pesar de todas
las incomodidades,
las traiciones de
la carne y sus
deseados pecados,
no quiere morir
tampoco quiere
un audífono
porque a veces, no es
necesario oír mejor,
porque a veces, es mejor
no saber
no desear saber los sonidos de la
lujuria
o los ruidos traicioneros de la guerra
mi abuela Josefina
con la tenacidad de Napoleón
ante todas las cosas,
prefiere la sordera,
la delicia de
sólo oír
lo que se quiere
oír
y tal vez
no se puede decir.

MY GRANDMOTHER

My grandmother
the radiant
Josefina,
who crossed
the Andean
cordillera
on foot and on mule,
who loved
late President Allende's
green eyes,
who is 84
and who in spite of every
discomfort,
betrayals of
the flesh and her
longed-for-sins,
does not wish to die,
or to wear
a hearing aid either,
because, sometimes, it's better
not to know,
not to want to know the sounds of
lechery
or the traitorous clamor of war.
My grandmother, Josefina,
with the tenacity of Napoleon
prefers above
all else
deafness,
the delight of
only hearing
what she wants
to hear
and perhaps
is unable to say.

JERUSALÉN DE LOS SILENCIOS

En un silencio traído,
en un caminar de sombra,
los judíos de Jerusalén
avanzan hacia las piedras:
cabizbajos, descalzos,
quieren llegar al muro
de sal y cielo,
encendidos de fe,
alegres,
incrustan papeles secretos,
dorados presagios entre las piedras.
Le piden a Dios
el derecho al aliento,
al aire,
rescatar las palabras,
el principio del verbo,
la vida,
tras las piedras.

JERUSALEM OF THE SILENCES

In an old worn silence,
walking among the shadows,
the Jews of Jerusalem
advance toward the stones:
heads bowed, barefoot,
they want to reach the wall
made of salt and heaven.
Bound by a deep faith,
happy,
they encrust secret papers,
golden portents among the stones.
They pray to God for
the right to breathe,
for air,
to recover words,
the origin of language,
life,
behind the stones.

ODESA

Y cuando te nombro
mi diminuta Sonia,
y cuando te pienso
adormecida asoleada,
se aparece
tu bisabuela
de Odessa
con algas en sus párpados,
con recetas
para curar el mal
de ojo y con ajos,
con las sedosas mantas
de percal,
te cubre.

Cuando te canto Sonia,
la escucho llegar
desesperada con los hijos de otros hijos,
con la guerra en sus ojos de sabia hacedora.

ODESSA

And when I say your name,
my little Sonia,
and when I think of you
falling asleep in the sun,
your great-grandmother
from Odessa
appears
with seaweed on her eyelids,
with recipes
to cure the evil eye;
and with garlic,
with handwoven, soft as
silk shawls,
she covers you.

When I sing to you, Sonia,
I hear her arrive
despairing with the children of other children,
with war in her eyes of a wise maker.

CANDELABROS

Mi abuela
Helena
la dama de Viena
la andariega danzante,
sólo llevó
de su ciudad
los candelabros
de plata,
el mantel familiar
y la palidez
de los candados
sepultados
en su falda
sangrante.

MOISÉS

Moisés añoró el desierto
y sus pozas invisibles.
Buscó en las grietas de la arena
la magia y la sed.
Añoró el refugio para esa despiadada
soledad del pueblo más solo.
Fue en el desierto,
entre los colores invisibles,
que nacieron las generaciones más antiguas.

CANDELABRAS

My grandmother
Helena,
the lady of Vienna,
the wandering dancer,
only brought
from her city
silver
candelabras,
the family linen
and the pallor
of padlocks
buried
under her bleeding
skirt.

R.S.

MOSES

Moses yearned for the desert
with its invisible wells.
He looked for magic and thirst
in the fissures of the sand.
He sought refuge for that merciless
solitude of the loneliest race.
It was in the desert,
among invisible colors,
that the oldest generations were born.

C.K.C.

PRIMAS

Mi madre murmuraba
al nombrarlas,
Julia, Silvia, Sonia,
Sonia, Julia, Silvia.
Eran nombres de ríos
nombres de mujeres hadas.
Eran mis primas,
mujeres conocidas,
de familia, sagradas.
Yo las amaba desde lejos
y desde cerca.

No sabíamos nada de ellas.
Poco se sabía del tiempo obstinado
de la guerra,
tan sólo ciertas claves,
un murmullo
como un suspiro.
Nos enviaban direcciones secretas,
jamás resueltas,
pistas falsas,
nombres invisibles.

Para las fiestas sagradas
había puestos vacíos
y mi padre, con una copa sagrada,
las nombraba,
Julia, Sonia, Silvia.

Yo llegué también a quererlas.
Me conformaba con
conocer su letra
en raídas postales de Viena, luego

COUSINS

My mother muttered
when she named them,
Julia, Silvia, Sonia,
Sonia, Julia, Silvia.
They were the names of rivers,
the names of fairies.
They were my cousins,
women we knew,
with whom we shared a history.
I loved them from a distance
and close by.

We know nothing about them.
Little was known about the obedient time
of war,
only certain clues,
a murmur,
a sigh.
They sent us encrypted addresses,
never deciphered,
false trails,
invisible names.

On holy days
there were empty seats
and my father, with his sacred cup,
invoked them,
Julia, Sonia, Silvia.

I also came to love them,
happy just
to see their handwriting
in threadbare postcards
from Vienna, then

Praga y
luego las ciudades de nombres austeros.

Mi abuela Helena,
taciturna,
sacaba sus fotografías que
parecían huesos color de ámbar,
brillando entre las ausencias.
De pronto,
casi cincuenta años
después,
llama el primo de Suecia,
y no puede dejar de recordar.

Nos contó,
mudo,
delgado entre la distancia,
que las había visto,
a esas primas:
Julia, Sonia, Silvia.
Las había encontrado
en el libro sagrado de
los muertos.
Las había buscado por
sus apellidos,
y sus travesías.

Habían sido trasladadas en aquellos
trenes de sombras
y calvas mujeres
cantando con sus trajes azules
a Terezin
para luego mandarlas a
Auschwitz
donde no hay olvidos,
donde no hay calendarios,

Prague and
later, the cities of austere names.

My grandmother, Helena,
taciturn,
took out her photographs that
resembled amber-colored bones,
shining among absences.
Suddenly,
almost fifty years
later,
the cousin from Sweden calls,
and he can't help but remember.

He told us,
mute,
ethereal in the distance,
that he had seen them,
those cousins:
Julia, Sonia, Silvia.
He had found them
in the Holy Book of
the dead.
He had searched for
their last names,
and their crossings.

They had been transferred to those
trains of shadows
and shorn women,
singing in their blue clothes,
to Terezin,
later to be sent to
Auschwitz,
where there is no forgetting,
where there are no calendars,

donde no hay memoria,
donde no hay voz,
donde las mujeres enmudecen,
son rapadas,
deliran
y hacen de sus cabezas los ceremoniales
de los pájaros muertos.

El primo de Suecia
las encontró.
Estaban muertas y vivas
o habían llegado en una tarde de ámbar
heridas y muertas.

Me dice rápidamente
que las mataron con el gas azul
y que eso es todo lo que se sabe de ellas.
Dice que se lo cuente a mi madre
también a la tía Regina.

Todas ellas
en Auschwitz
y no sé cómo nombrarlas
y no sé cómo recordarlas.

La ira se confunde con mi aullido.
Las reconozco
Sonia, Julia, Silvia.
Ya no puedo nombrarlas
y las veo sajadas en esos bosques
de mariposas muertas
y pienso que no merezco esta vida
sin ellas.

Le digo a mi madre

where there is no memory,
where there is no voice,
where women keep silent,
are shorn,
are delirious
and carry on their heads the rituals
of dead birds.

The cousins from Sweden
found them.
They were dead and alive
or they arrived in an afternoon of amber,
wounded and dead.

He tells me hurriedly
that they killed them with blue gas
and that is all he knows about them.
He asks me to tell this to my mother
and also to Aunt Regina.

All of them
in Auschwitz,
and I don't know how to name them,
and I don't know how to remember them.

Anger blends with my screams.
I recognize them
Sonia, Julia, Silvia.
I cannot name them anymore,
I see them severed in those forests
of dead butterflies
and I think I do not deserve this life
without them.

I tell my mother

y a mi abuela, que ha quedado
olvidada en el sur,
que no
debemos buscarlas.
Que no estipulemos falsos
presagios;
que ahí están;
que al llegar
las hicieron arder;
que sus huesitos fueron colocados
sin nombre en los hornos diminutos
de la muerte.
Me nublo toda al contarte esta historia
y sólo la cuento en un poema
porque no puedo decírsela a nadie.
No quiero oír cosas como:
"Otra vez los judíos y sus memorias."
"Eso pasó hace años."
"Yo no sé nada del asunto."
Así hablaban cuando se desapareció el vecino,
el abuelo,
sus nietos pequeños.

Esta noche
gira y gira en mi cabeza
como un atado de amapolas
muertas.
Ya sé dónde están Julia, Sonia, Silvia.
Iré a navegar esos prados.
Mi pasión besará esos céspedes
esperando encontrar sus labios.

Julia, Sonia, Silvia,
no morirán entre los alambres.

and my grandmother, who has remained
forgotten in the South,
that we should not
search for them,
not to imagine false
omens;
that they are here;
that upon their arrival
they made them burn;
their tiny bones were placed
without names in the minuscule ovens
of death.

I feel distressed when I tell you this story
and I can only say it in a poem
because I cannot tell it to anybody.
I don't want to hear things like
"Again, the Jews and their memories."
"That happened years ago."
"I don't know anything about that."
That is how they talked when the neighbor,
the grandfather,
his small grandchildren
disappeared.

Tonight
all of this turns in my head
like a gathering of wilted
poppies.
I don't know where Julia, Sonia, Silvia are.
I shall navigate those meadows.
My passion will kiss the grass
waiting to meet their lips.

Julia, Sonia, Silvia,
you shall not die among barbed wires.

No serán más los judíos ocultos
sin cabellos y sin lenguaje.

Yo regresaré a los campos
para regarlos con rezos y agua santa.
Te regalaré un cuaderno, Julia,
un abanico, Sonia,
un soplo de luz, Silvia.
Primas mías, primas hermanas mías.
Familia que nunca llegó a ser amada más.
No quiero engaños para vuestros nombres.
No quiero que nadie hable
por vuestros nombres.
Pido un segundo, un siglo de paz
y memoria
para todas
las judías muertas,
las gitanas,
las mujeres de Bosnia.
Todas se llaman
Julia, Silvia, Sonia
y son mías.

You shall no longer be the hidden Jews
without hair or language.

I will return to the fields
to sprinkle them with prayers and holy water.
I shall give you a notebook, Julia,
a fan, Sonia,
a breath of light, Silvia.
My cousins, my blood cousins,
family that could no longer be loved.
I don't want lies for your names.
I don't want anybody to speak
on your behalf.
I ask for a second, a century of peace
and memory
for all
the dead Jews,
the gypsies,
the women of Bosnia.
They are all named
Julia, Silvia, Sonia
and they are mine.

L.N.

1939

I.

Supo ella seducir al destino,
vaticinar la hora de la huida
en 1939, vestida con el traje
de noche y la dicha
en los umbrales del temeroso
puerto de Hamburgo,
navegó,
resuelta a la vida,
hasta los mares del sur.

En 1938 los ventanales
de su casa de agua y piedra
resistieron el inmensurable
horror de aquella noche
de los cristales rotos.

Ella, mi abuela
me enseñó a reconocer el
paisaje del peligro,
las trizaduras del miedo
el rostro impenetrable
de las mujeres
que huyen,
acusadas,
audaces en su deseo de vivir.

1939

I.

She knew how to seduce her destiny,
predict the time of flight
in 1939, dressed in garments
of night and happiness
at the threshold of a fearful
Hamburg Harbor
resolved to live,
she sailed
to Southern seas.

In 1938, the windows
of her house of water and stone
resisted the extreme
horror of that night
of broken crystals.

She, my grandmother,
taught me to recognize
the landscape of danger,
the shards of fear,
the impenetrable faces
of women,
fleeing,
accused,
audacious in their will to live.

II.

Helena Broder,
fabricó un universo
de papeles, frágiles embarcaciones
de poemas clandestinos y
apuntes por hacerse,
direcciones discretas,
livianas de equipaje,
como un ángel,
frágil y delicado,
aunque lista para embarcarse nuevamente.

Sobreviví junto a ella
y agradecí el obsequio de su presencia.

II.

Helena Broder,
created a domain
of papers, fragile vessels,
clandestine poems and
notes to be made,
discreet addresses.
With little baggage,
like a frail and ancient
angel,
she arrived,
although ready to embark again.

I survived next to her
and I was thankful for the gift of her presence.

CREÍ QUE ERAS UN ÁNGEL, HELENA

I.

Creí que eras un
ángel
a tientas por los
corredores,
una huésped
extraña a
tus propias pertenencias.

Creí que eras un ángel
que reza mientras atraviesa
corredores vacíos,
vidas perplejas y cantos como rezos cálidos.
Pero eras tú, abuela mía,
vagando por la noche
por tu casa de la memoria,
una cámara secreta,
escribiendo palabras que se deslizan
en el silencio
que desvarías ajena tras los cuartos quebrados.
¿A quién buscabas tan leve y pequeña
con tu camisón blanco
y una linterna diminuta?

Creí que eras un ángel
y jugué a descubrir cada uno
de tus mensajes,
mensajera de la vida breve,
de la memoria frágil,
jardinera de flores nocturnas.

I THOUGHT YOU WERE AN ANGEL, HELENA

I.

I thought you were
an angel
feeling your way
in the hallways,
a strange
guest among
your own belongings.

I thought you were an angel,
praying, while walking
the empty hallways,
perplexed lives and songs like soft prayers.
But it was you, grandmother of mine,
wandering at night,
in your house of memory,
a secret chamber,
writing words that
glide into silence,
delirious, facing the shattered rooms.
Who were you looking for, so light and small,
with your white nightgown
and your tiny lantern?

I thought you were an angel
and I played trying to uncover
each one of your messages,
messenger of brief life,
frail memory,
gardener of nocturnal flowers.

II.

Juqué con tus rizos blancos
con tus cabellos de malva
y de humo.
Reposé mis dedos en los surcos
de tu rostro
detrás del cual
encontré montes claros,
lunas sagradas y
la permanencia tenaz
de este invierno
y eras un ángel
alucinado.

II.

I played with your white curls
with your mauve
and smoky hair.
I rested my fingers in the furrows
of your face,
behind which
I found transparent hills,
sacred moons and
the tenacious permanence
of this winter,
and you were an
hallucinated angel.

EL CUADERNO DE LOS SUEÑOS

Has desatado tus cabellos abuela como lo haces todas las noches, para comenzar con el rito del sueño. Dejas la almohada de plumas reposando sobre tu cama de felpas rojizas. Extiendes el camisón de algodón recién planchado. Te miramos con extrañeza, pero a la vez felices que todas las noches recorres los mismos lugares, las pequeñas travesías de tu mesa redonda a la cama reposada que aguarda ansiosa la llegada de tu cuerpo tan solo. Ya nadie te abraza por las noches, abuela, tan sólo el recuerdo o lo que olvidas, porque aquel mundo querido nunca fue tuyo y el que tienes ahora no lo reconoces. Sólo aguardas la mañana, los periódicos de la guerra, las cartas de la Cruz Roja que no llegan.

THE NOTEBOOK OF DREAMS

Grandmother, you have untied your hair as you do every night to begin the ritual of sleep. You leave the feather pillow lying on your plush red bed and spread out the freshly ironed cotton nightgown. We look at you with surprise, but happy that every night you visit the same places, the short trips to your round table and restful bed, anxiously waiting the arrival of only your body. Nobody embraces you any longer at night, grandmother, only your memory or what you choose to forget, because that beloved world was never yours, and you do not accept the one you have now. You just wait for morning, for newspapers from the war, and Red Cross letters that never arrive.

LAS PALABRAS DE HELENA BRODER, 1945

Al anochecer
hablabas con
las palomas
extraviadas,
las palomas mensajeras
que regresaban impávidas
sin noticias de tus muertos.
Eran tus palabras hilos bordados,
ceremonias huidizas.

Al anochecer, te oigo.
No sé si rezas o cantas.
Tu cabello es una brisa
donde se posan pétalos maléficos,
casas y ciudades vacías,
zapatos olvidados,
botas que aprisionan
y siempre las pisadas precisas
y el silencio más ajeno
tras ésas, las pisadas.
Tan sólo la memoria
que se resiste al olvido
se posa frente a ti
como una dama ceremoniosa,
frente al glorioso pasado
de esa Europa central
donde los judíos alaban
la permanencia de las melodías.
Ahora que nada queda,
Helena Broder
y es imposible reconocer a tus muertos,
eres una mujer sola frente al balcón
y la noches.
Las palomas conocen tu secreto
y sollozan en tu cabellera.

THE WORDS OF HELENA BRODER, 1945

At nightfall
you used to speak with
the lost
birds,
the messenger doves,
that returned unperturbed,
without news of your dead.
Your words were embroidered threads,
elusive ceremonies.

At nightfall, I hear you.
I don't know if you are praying or singing.
Your hair is a breeze
where evil petals rest,
houses and empty cities,
forgotten shoes,
tight boots
and always clear footsteps
and the most deafening silence
that follows the heavy ones.
Only memory, resisting oblivion,
rests before you
like an elegant lady,
facing the glorious past
of that central Europe
where Jews praised
the permanence of
melodies.
Now that nothing remains,
Helena Broder,
and it is impossible to recognize your dead,
you are alone before your balcony
and the night.
Only the doves know your secret
and sob in your hair.   L.N.

MIRIAM

Mi hermano y yo
fuimos los testigos de Dios
sobre el desierto.
El anotaba la vida
sobre las piedras,
yo jugaba a imaginar
el agua sobre la arena,
áspera y oscura.

Mi hermano fue el elegido,
recibió el don de todas las posibles palabras,
a Dios le gustaban sus pasos
y su aliento.

Dios se enfadó ante mi deseo
de también ser peregrina como mi pueblo,
me llenó la piel
de escamas, de peces muertos.

Entre la oscurísima oscuridad,
me quedé en un calabozo
y en la luz del jardín,
de todo desierto,
las mujeres me esperaban.
Cantaban mi nombre.

De pronto,
me di cuenta
que tan sólo mi hermano
escribía
entre las piedras los dictados de Dios,
ese Dios que me había dejado tan muda y tan sola
en aquella vasta soledad del Sinaí.

MIRIAM

My brother and I
were God's witnesses
in the desert.
He inscribed life
on the rocks,
and I played at imagining
water on the sand,
bitter and dark.

My brother was the chosen one
he received the gift of language.
His demeanor and
courage pleased God.

Angered over my desire
to be a pilgrim just like my people,
God covered my skin
with scales of dead fish.

Amid the most opaque darkness
I remained in a dungeon
and in the pure light of the garden,
of the whole desert,
the women waited for me
singing my name.

Suddenly
I realized
that only my brother
wrote
the dictations of God amid the rocks,
that God who had left me so silent and alone
in the vast solitude of the Sinai.

Me quedé sola
con mis mujeres
sin nombre,
sin historia,
sin Dios.
Me llamo Miriam,
canto,
otorgo palabras.

I stayed behind
with my women
without names,
without history,
without God.
My name is Miriam,
I sing,
I grant words.

M.B.G.

MOTHERS AND CHILDREN

ESCÚCHAME ANA FRANK

A John

Óyeme Ana Frank
¿en verdad creías que todos los hombres eran buenos?
mientras muy a lo cerca
quemaban los bosques
que se entrecortaban en tus ojos de pozo blando.
mientras no orinabas hasta después del atardecer
porque el orín de una niña judía
delataba a los desdentados gendarmes
acechando la fragilidad de tu memoria.

Ana,
¿me decías que quedaban hombres buenos?
que no te acusaban jamás
mientras te traían lápices, cuadernos y espejismos desmayados.

Escúchame de una vez Ana Frank
parece que te bastaba asomarte entre las rendijas de la ratonera
acomodar tu insomniado pelo
mirar al cielo,
ver y no ver botellas azules como peces, marcando el rumbo de
       las nubes
despertarte con los silbidos de algún lobo
pero tú, siempre tú
seguías enamorada
porque tus senos crecían como un humo delgado y suave.

Ana Frank
nunca te leí tan lúcida
con tu cuaderno bajo el brazo desnutrido
con los afiches de Greta Garbo
y entre las palabras
"I still believe that people are really good at heart."

LISTEN TO ME ANNE FRANK

For John

Listen to me Anne Frank
did you really believe that all men were good?
even though very close by
they were burning the forests
that crackled in the tender pools of your eyes.
even though you didn't urinate until after dark
because the urine of a Jewish girl
would alert the toothless guards
waiting to ambush your fragile memory.

Anne,
so you kept telling me that there were still good men
that they never denounced you
while they were bringing you pencils, notebooks and sickly illusions.

Listen to me for once Anne Frank
it seems it was enough for you to look out between the bars of your
rattrap
to arrange your sleepless hair
to gaze at the sky
to see and not see blue bottles like fish, marking the direction of
        the clouds
to wake up at the whistle of some Big Bad Wolf
but you, you were
always enamored
because your breasts were growing delicate and smooth as smoke.

Anne Frank
I never read you so lucid
with your notebook under your undernourished arm
the notebook with the pictures of Greta Garbo
and among the words:
"I still believe that people are really good at heart."

Entonces alguien escuchó que hoy habían quemado árboles y judíos
tú decías que:
"I must uphold my ideals for perhaps the time will come when I shall
be able to carry them out."

Ana Frank
nunca te supe tan valiente
cuando la embarcación de necios verdugos
cortó burlonamente tus orejas
jugaron con tus ovarios recién nacidos
juegos de dagas y sangre fermentada
raparon tu cabello
para reírse mejor
sellaron tus ojos huecos.

Pero tu boca no se hizo un desierto en la mudez de los tiranos
y yo pensaba en el desierto de Atacama y una niña sacando una mano
entre los manantiales
y pensaba en Lonquén y en la vergüenza de los mentirosos
(Lonquén es un horno como el horno en que murió tu madre y todos
los hermanos, compañeros)

Ana Frank
Contéstame desde la tumba descompuesta entre los gusanos
¿en verdad creías en los hombres buenos
mientras te desatabas el cabello, descalza pisabas el aire
y siempre mirabas al cielo?

Then someone heard that on that day they had burned trees and Jews
and you were saying:
"I must uphold my ideals for perhaps the time will come when I shall
be able to carry them out."

Anne Frank
I never knew you so courageous
when the crew of stupid executioners
slashed your ears as a joke
played games with your newly awakened ovaries
games of daggers and clotted blood
they shaved your head
for greater amusement
sealed up your empty eyes.

But your mouth did not dry up like a desert amid the muteness of
the tyrants
(and I was thinking of the desert of Atacama and a little girl
pulling a hand from the waters of a spring)
and I was thinking of Lonquén and of the shamefulness of the liars
(Lonquén is an oven like the oven where your mother died, all your
brothers and companions.)

Anne Frank
answer me from your decayed tomb amid the worms
did you really believe there were good men
even as you loosened your hair, and walked barefoot through the
air, still gazing at the sky?

LA DESAPARECIDA VI

Madre mía
sé que me llamas
y que tus yemas
cubren esas heridas, abiertas
muertas y resucitadas
una y otra vez.

Cuando vendada
me llevan a los
cuartos del
delirio.
Es tu voz
nueva,
iluminada,
que oigo
tras los golpes
desangrados
como los árboles
de un
patio de
verdugos.

Madre mía
yo duermo entre
tus brazos
y me asusto
ante los puñales
pero
tú me recoges
desde un fondo
lleno de dagas y serpientes.

DISAPPEARED WOMAN VI

Mother
I know you are calling me
and that your fingertips
are covering those wounds, open
dead and re-opened
over and over again.

When I am blindfolded
they carry me to the
rooms of
delirium.
It is your voice
new,
luminous,
that I hear
after the bloodletting
blows
like trees
in a
patio of
assassins.

Mother
I sleep in
your arms
and feel frightened
by the knives
but
you gather me up
from the abyss
filled with daggers and serpents.

DELANTALES DE HUMO

Abismada y llena de pesadumbres
aladas,
la sangre se extiende,
danza y recorre el
delantal de humo,
se traslada hasta el
comienzo de mis
piernas y
enloquecida no me obedece,
sólo rueda destemplada
invade los colores
de mi piel
me trastorna de
carmesí
y entre el pavor del silencio,
entre la lejanía del
espanto,
se apodera de mis muertos y de mis vivos
marchita se despide
robándome a un niño
muerto
perdido entre los coágulos de mareas envenenadas.

APRONS OF SMOKE

Somber and full of winged
nightmares,
blood spreads out,
dances and overruns the
apron of smoke,
moves to the
edge of my legs and
maddened does not obey me,
but flows untimely
invades the colors
of my skin
deranges me with
crimson
and between the horror of silence
the distance of
terror,
takes possession of my dead and my living ones
faded takes leave
robbing me of a child
dead
lost among clots of venomous tides.

C.F.

Cuando me enseñó su fotografía
me dijo
ésta es mi hija
aún no llega a casa
hace diez años que no llega
pero ésta es su fotografía
¿Es muy linda no es cierto?
es una estudiante de filosofía
y aquí está cuando tenía
catorce años
e hizo su primera
comunión
almidonada, sagrada.
ésta es mi hija
es tan bella
todos los días converso con ella
ya nunca llega tarde a casa, yo por eso la reprocho
mucho menos
pero la quiero tantísimo
ésta is mi hija
todas las noches me despido de ella
la beso
y me cuesta no llorar
aunque sé que no llegará
tarde a casa
porque tú sabes, hace años que
no regresa a casa
yo quiero mucho a esta foto
la miro todos los días
me parece ayer cuando
era un angelito de plumas en mis manos
y aquí está toda hecha una dama
una estudiante de filosofía
una desaparecida
pero no es cierto que es tan linda,
que tiene un rostro de angel.
que parece que estuviera viva?

When she showed me her photograph
she said,
This is my daughter.
She still hasn't come home.
She hasn't come home in ten years.
But this is her photograph.
Isn't it true that she is very pretty?
She is a philosophy student
and here she is when she was
fourteen years old
and had her first
communion,
starched, sacred.
This is my daughter.
She is so pretty.
I talk to her every day.
She no longer comes home late, and this is why I reproach her
much less.
But I love her so much.
This is my daughter.
Every night I say goodbye to her.
I kiss her
and it's hard for me not to cry
even though I know she will not come
home late
because as you know, she has not come
home for years.
I love this photo very much.
I look at it every day.
It seems that only yesterday
she was a little feathered angel in my arms
and here she looks like a young lady,
a philosophy student, another disappeared.
But isn't it true that she is so pretty,
that she has an angel's face,
that it seems as if she were alive?

Una mujer aguarda a sus muertos, en un comedor
insensato. Aulla esos nombres como los dados de la muerte; se
resfriega los ojos y pide verlos mejor,
decirles cosas como el color del cielo en los parques,
o el porqué de las lluvias en una mirada.
Una mujer habla de la muerte como si fuera una vagabunda en
rotaciones ancladas.
Una mujer conversa con la muerte en
un comedor de sillas mancas, de
tenedores carmesíes, un cuchillo
solitario
desfila en la penumbra.
Una mujer aguarda a sus muertos.

A woman waits for her dead in a useless
dining room. She howls those names
like the dice of death; she clears her eyes
and asks to see them better,
to tell them things like the color of the sky
in the parks,
or the reason for her tear-drenched look.
A woman talks about death as if it were a vagabond
moving in a tethered circle.
A woman converses with death in
a dining room of maimed chairs,
scarlet-colored forks, and a
solitary knife
marching in the semi-darkness.
A woman waits for her dead.

C.K.C.

SONIDOS

José Daniel
oye con el alma
y habla con el aire.
Por eso repite alucinado
las ondulaciones del agua
y abre sus manos de mago
para acariciarla
tirar las piedras
al río
al mar,
a la orilla de los tiempos
como si estuviera nombrando
litorales
como si su voz fuera
un muelle que brilla
en cada sílaba
en cada agua que pronuncia.

SOUNDS

José Daniel
hears with his soul
and speaks with the air.
Beguiled, he mimics
the undulations of the water,
opens his magician's hands
to caress it,
to toss stones
at the river,
the sea,
the shore of time
as if he were dubbing
coastlines,
as if his voice were
a pier gleaming
in each syllable
in each body of water he pronounces.

C.F.

BUSQUÉ UN HUERTO DE HUESOS

Vengo a buscar estos
huesos,
se parecían a la piel vencida
de los animales difuntos,
pero los quiero
para mi huerto.
Para amarrarlos
junto a los rosales.
Le digo
que son mis huesos,
los huesos de mi hijo,
Julián,
quiero que conozcan
la lluvia
los sueños
de la paz,
por eso, señor, me los
vengo a llevar
aquí en mis faldas,
esos huesos quiero
yo
porque
ya dejaron de ser suyos
porque esa vida jamás
fue suya.
Porque Ud. sólo supo hablar de los rostros de la
muerte
porque no tiene nada que ver con la vida.
Deme mis huesos, capitán.

I SOUGHT A GARDEN OF BONES

I've come seeking these
bones,
and though they call to mind the defeated
flesh of dead animals,
I want them
for my garden,
to string them up
beside the rose bushes.
I'm telling you
they are my bones,
the bones of my son,
Julian,
and I want them to know
the rain,
the dreams
of peace,
therefore, señor, I've come here
to carry off these bones
I love
in the pleats of my skirt,
because
they have ceased
being yours
because that life never
was yours.
Because you knew only how to talk about death's faces
because you and life have nothing in common.
Give me my bones, my captain.

AMSTERDAM

Todos vienen a visitar
mi casa
soy Ana Frank
una niña judía que
creía
en los hombres buenos.
Estoy muerta
desde que incendiaron
mi pelo anochecido.
Estoy muerta
desde que me robaron
mi diario de mi vida.
Sin embargo
todos estos visitantes
acuden a mí con frecuencia
y no me ven.
Tampoco a mi mamá
silenciosa,
sometida,
parecida a un pájaro errante
protegiéndome de mis sueños
acarreando muy de madrugada unos balones de agua.

Soy Ana Frank
tengo trece años
pero también miles de años.
Tengo el olor a humo y vejeces
que cubren los rostros del miedo.

AMSTERDAM

Everyone comes to visit
my house
I am Anne Frank
a Jewish girl who
believed
in the goodness of men.
I am dead
since they burned my dark hair,
I am dead
since they stole
my diary.
And yet
all these visitors
who frequently call on me
don't see me.
Not even my silent,
submissive
mother,
resembling
an errant bird,
protecting me from my dreams,
lugging buckets of water at the crack of dawn.

I am Anne Frank
I am thirteen years old
but I am also thousands of years old.
I smell of smoke and old age
covering the faces of fear.

Algunos visitantes
dicen que
el rostro no es de
una mujer judía
pero soy judía.
¿Aún no lo sospechan?

En este anexo
derramé un collar de palabras
aprendí a hurtadillas a contemplar el cielo
también con gran dificultad
aprendí a amarrarme los zapatos.

Soy Ana Frank
estoy muerta.
Pero para Uds. viva.
Aún tengo tanto miedo
no puedo con mi cuerpo
aplastado por la
neblina de las infamias
si tan sólo pudiera llegar
a la claridad,
para afirmarme con la luz
de una flor
si tan sólo
pudiera ver el rostro de mi madre.

Some visitors
say
my face is not that of
a Jewish girl,
but I am Jewish.
Is it that they don't even suspect it?

In this annex
I strung out a necklace of words
I learned by stealth to contemplate the sky
also with great difficulty
I learned to tie my shoes.

I am Anne Frank
I am dead.
But for you I am alive.
Even though I am terribly afraid
I can't be with my body
crushed under
the fog thick with infamies.
If only I could reach
the sunlit clearing
to affirm myself with the light
of a flower,
if only
I could see the face of my mother.

R.S.

LAS MUJERES DE SARAJEVO

En Sarajevo
nieva,
acercándose a los caminos
dejando su caminar de sangre
su transparencia de mirada ahuecada
nieva en Sarajevo,
y los muertos no saben dónde guarecerse.
Nieva en Sarajevo y el invierno es como un corazón
entre las sombras negras.
Muy a lo lejos
las pisadas de los vivos
haciendo alianzas con los
muertos.
Un dedo del muerto
dibujando corazones.

II.

En Sarajevo
este invierno
las mujeres acarician el
arpa de la noche.
Sueñan con las frutas del sur.
los arpegios,
se alimentan de ese sonido tan hondo
del piano
en el medio de la noche que rumia
que se desplaza
para ahuyentar a los muertos.

THE WOMEN OF SARAJEVO

In Sarajevo
the snow weaves fragile paths,
approaching the roads,
leaving its bloody steps,
the transparency of its hollow gaze.
It snows in Sarajevo,
the dead do not know where to seek shelter.
It snows in Sarajevo and the winter is like a heart
among the black shadows.
Very far away...very close by
the footsteps of the living
making alliances with the
dead.
A finger from the corpse
drawing hearts.

II.

In Sarajevo
this winter
the women caress the
harps of the night,
the eyelids of the night.
They dream with fruits from the South,
arpeggios,
they feed themselves with that very deep sound
from the piano
in the midst of the night that ruminates,
that moves
to chase away the dead.

III.

Este invierno nevará copiosamente en Sarajevo
sospechosamente nevará en Sarajevo
los vivos sabrán cómo y por qué hacer el amor,
alguien escribirá versos sobre la escarcha
porque no podrán hablar
porque nadie los verá tras la transparencia
porque la nieve es un silencio sagrado.

IV.

En Sarajevo
los niños también mueren
y no mueren en accidentes de autos.
Nieva tan copiosamente
y los muertos no saben dónde guarecerse
las mujeres acarician
las arpas
de la noche.

III.

This winter it will snow copiously in Sarajevo.
Suspiciously it will snow in Sarajevo.
The living will know how and why they make love,
somebody will write poetry on the frost
because they will not be able to speak,
because no one will see them in their transparency,
because snow is a sacred silence.

IV.

In Sarajevo
the children also die
and they do not die in automobile accidents.
It snows so copiously
and the dead do not know where to seek shelter.
The women caress
the harps
of the night.

VIDA NUEVA

a Enrique Lihn

Sonia Helena
nada se pierde
con vivir
escoge
la imperfección
del azar
los ritmos circundantes
de divagaciones
y profecías
ensaya y practica
la vulnerabilidad
sé ambigua
con el destino
sé generosa con
el tirano
con el austero en el amor.
enséñales a
extender una mano
y conservar la ilusión
de lo profundo,
esa es la felicidad
sin premura
aprende a escuchar a los muertos,
y sus pasos como la marcha del tango.

Sé cálida
con los que lloran,
con los exiliados
los que emigran
y también
déjales saber
que llevan el paisaje de
la patria en sus miradas.

NEW LIFE

to Enrique Lihn and Sonia Helena

Sonia Helena
nothing is lost
by living.
Choose
the imperfection
of chance,
the surrounding rhythms
of digressions
and prophecies.
Try and practice
vulnerability.
Be ambiguous
with destiny.
Be generous with
the tyrant,
austere in love.
Teach them to
stretch out a hand
and hang on to the illusion
of the deep,
that is happiness
without a hurry.
Learn to listen to the dead,
and their steps like the march of the tango.

Be warm
with those who cry,
with the exiled,
those who migrate
from all cities
and also let them know
that they carry the landscape of
the nation in their eyes.

Sonia Helena,
nada se pierde con
vivir.
Como decía Enrique,
ensaya,
vive la vida como si
fuera siempre un regreso
no tengas prisa
porque tenemos todo el tiempo del mundo.

En los momentos
del insomnio
cuando navegas y eres
una sombra trastornada,
elige la poesía
porque ella como los
rezos sabrán
ser tu ángel protector
y el verso será para ti
una pluma
en el labio
de tu Dios.

Más que sobrevivir,
escoge vivir
con todos sus riesgos siniestros
hazles ofrenda a los pájaros de la tierra
al verdor
al tronco del abismo,
cultiva los ritos, pero más que nada las ceremonias del amor,
esconde todos los amuletos, la envidia y la posible mezquindad.
No seas demasiado
cautelosa
o muy severa contigo misma
ni sueñes con grandes
éxitos.

Sonia Helena,
nothing is lost in
living.
As Enrique used to say,
try,
live life as if it were always a return
the birthplace of flat waves.
Do not hurry
because we have all the time in the world.

During times
of insomnia,
when you sail and you are
a disturbed shadow,
choose poetry
because it, as well as
prayer, will know how
to be your guardian angel
and verse will be for you
a feather
on the lip
of your God.

More than to survive,
choose to live life
with all its sinister risks.
Make offerings to the birds of the earth,
to the greenness,
to the trunk of the abyss.
Foster rites, the ceremonies of love.
Hide all the amulets, the envy and possible pettiness.
Do not be too
cautious,
or too severe with yourself,
or wish for great
achievements.

No olvides que
la felicidad
es tan sólo
una mano,
un suspiro,
obsequiar
una violeta.

Nada se pierde
con vivir
Sonia Helena
trata
Sonia Helena,
hija mía
escoge la vida.

Do not forget that
happiness
is only
a hand,
a sigh,
to give
a violet.

Nothing is lost
in living
Sonia Helena,
with trying,
Sonia Helena,
daughter, friend,
choose life.

MUÑECA DE TRAPO

I.
Esta muñeca es para ti,
Sonia Helena,
de lana revoltosa y gris,
de brazos pequeños
pero aún capaces
de recoger mariposas
y llorar desde los
asombros.

II.
Desde Chiloé,
tierra de meicas
y mujeres de ojos abiertos,
desde la lana hechizada
labrada por las
manos de mujeres
con manos de diosas y pordioseras,
te traje esta muñeca
Sonia Helena,
la muñeca de las niñas pobres,
para que tú
también
la arrulles
en los idiomas
inventados,
para que entiendas
de asperezas
y la suavidad
de las cosas
del amor.

RAG DOLL

I.
This doll is for you,
Sonia Helena,
made of frolicking and gray wool,
with small arms
but still capable
of catching butterflies
and crying out in
awe.

II.
From Chiloé,
land of healers
and women with open eyes,
from the magical yarn
embroidered by
the hands of women
by the hands of goddesses and beggars,
I brought you this doll
Sonia Helena,
the doll of poor children,
so that you
may also
lull it to sleep
in made up
languages,
so you can understand
about the harshness
and softness
of the objects
of love.

Sonia Helena
ten esta muñeca
de trapo,
de pelo canoso,
de una infancia entre las arcillas
y la oscuridad.
Quiero que seas la guardiana
de la Pancha,
que la cubras
y que no confundas
jamás el privilegio
de tus sábanas de seda.

Sonia Helena
take this rag
doll,
with graying hair,
from a childhood of clays
and darkness.
I want you to be Pancha's
guardian,
to cover her
and never mistake
the privilege
of your silk sheets.

SADAKO SASAKI

I.

Ya nadie reconoce
a Sadako Sasaki
invisible, bordada por cuentas
amarillas,
ya nadie tiene paciencia
para Sadako Sasaki
con sus delantales de humo
con su cabellos traslúcidos, empañados
de fuegos calcinados.

II.

¿Saben que Sadako Sasaki
era una dulce niña de
Hiroshima?
Tenía cabellos de duende,
vestía trajes transparentes como la piel del amor,
quiso desafiar a la muerte
con volantines azules.

III.

Entonces llegaron las llamas súbitas,
incendiaron las chimeneas del cielo,
los niños quedaron inmóviles en los juegos de la fe,
para siempre como las cosas de la guerra
y el silencio era como una navaja rapando la felicidad.

SADAKO SASAKI

I.

Nobody recognizes
Sadako Sasaki
invisible, framed by yellow
beads
nobody has patience
for Sadako Sasaki
with her pinafores of smoke
her translucent hair burnt
to ash by the fires.

II.

Do you know that Sadako Sasaki
was a sweet, gentle girl in
Hiroshima?
She had magical, wild hair,
she wore clear dresses like the skin of love,
she wanted to defy death
with blue kites.

III.

Then the sudden flames arrived
they set fires in the chimneys of the sky,
children remained forever still in
the games of faith like all things of war
and the silence was like a knife shaving away happiness.

IV.

Todos los niños de Hiroshima
visitan a Sadako Sasaki
en Hiroshima, en el universo olvidadizo
en un monumento olvidadizo
porque Hiroshima es la zona,
el abismo oscurecido
donde la muerte aún visita
endemoniando los
parajes de los niños.

¿Y dónde están los niños
de Hiroshima?
¿Quién los ha visto con
los rostros despavoridos?
Quiero encontrar a Sadako Sasaki
quiero encontrar a Ana Frank
quiero besar a los niños de la guerra
que nunca hicieron las guerras.

IV.

All the children of Hiroshima
visit Sadako Sasaki
in Hiroshima, in the forgotten universe
in a forgotten monument
because Hiroshima is the place,
the blackened abyss
where death still visits
haunting the sites
of children.

And where are the children
of Hiroshima?
Who has seen them with
their terrified faces?
I want to find Sadako Sasaki
I want to find Anne Frank
I want to kiss the children of war
who never made war.

                                        M.B.G.

PREGUNTAS

No reposaré en mis preguntas,
el recuerdo se perfila como una viajera errante.
Abuela, cuéntame de aquellos campos
donde los niños se vestían con el tatuaje de las
estrellas.

Insisto en preguntar
de aquel tiempo donde yo no estuve,
de aquellas estaciones sin calendarios,
de aquellas praderas donde las mariposas
parecían muertas en un silencio de
nieves muertas.

Abuela, ¿quién era Julia?
¿Dónde estaba tu casa?
¿Quién se quedó con tu jardín de lilas
con tu canasta de fresas?

En vano las preguntas,
como una piel agrietada,
recorren la historia de un tiempo sin tiempo
donde los hombres cercaban a los niños
en un jardín de alambres
con sus estrellas doradas
dibujándose en la luz
de las mariposas.

Abuela, cuéntame de tu memoria
cuando la noche era un vértigo nublado,
cuando no les temías a los fantasmas
pero sí a los hombres
vestidos de oscuridad.

QUESTIONS

I will not rest easy with my questions,
memory's profile is like a vagabond woman.
Grandmother, tell me about those camps
where children were clothed in tattoos made of
stars.

I insist upon asking
about a time that I did not inhabit,
about those seasons without calendars,
about those meadows where butterflies
seemed dead in the silence of
frozen snow.

Grandmother, who was Julia?
Where was your house?
Who ended up with your lilac garden
and your basket of strawberries?

In vain the questions,
like cracked skin,
traverse a vanishing history of a time without time
where men imprisoned children
in a barbed-wire garden
with their golden stars
sketched among the light
of the butterflies.

Grandmother, tell me from your memory
when the night was a vertiginous cloud,
when you didn't fear ghosts
but the men
cloaked in darkness.

SONIA HELENA II

Sonia Helena
la risa es como el aletear
de golondrinas,
como un salto de delfín enamorado.
La risa sirve para alisar las tristezas
inciertas,
para imaginar
los presagios color violeta.

Sonia Helena
hija mía,
amada mía,
amiga de las más diminutas historias,
no sé qué obsequiarte,
más de lo que soy
y lo que no puedo ser,
pero aquí te entrego
mi corazón como un desierto en calma.

Te obsequio mi voz.

SONIA HELENA II

Sonia Helena
laughter is like the fluttering
of swallows,
the leap of a dolphin in love.
Laughter serves to smooth
uncertain sorrows,
to imagine
violet-colored omens.

Sonia Helena
my daughter,
my love,
friend of tiny fairy tales,
I don't know what to leave to you,
more than what I am
and what I cannot be,
yet here I give you
my heart like a desert at peace.

I leave you my voice.

C.K.C.

EXILE

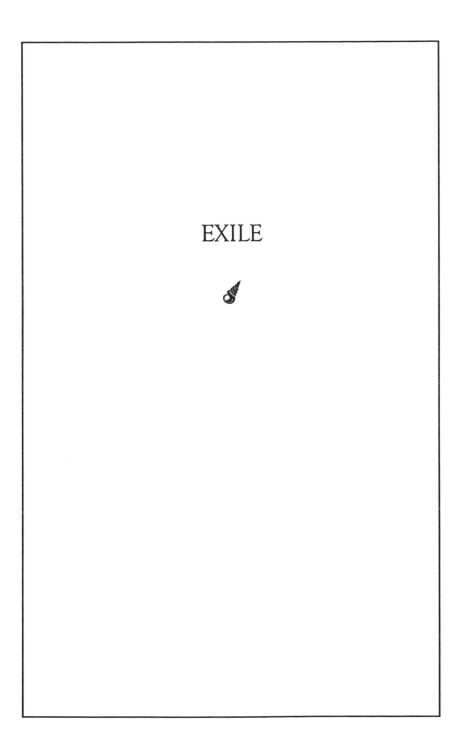

ESTADOS UNIDOS

Estados Unidos,
yo no invoco tu nombre
en vano,
ni te acuso por
desvirginar tantas estrellas
sólo me adhiero
a tus inmensas soledades
y entiendo que no es tu culpa
el haber inventado la vida en
ready-made
ni los anocheceres dorados
de Miss Monroe.
Aunque confiésate
que gozabas de la triste enfermedad
de los pueblos mansos
y trepaste hasta la vía andina
para llenarte de cobres, cromosomas, de fusil.
Pero pensándolo bien,
ahora al pasearme por Managua, San Salvador,
por la Avenida Providencia en Santiago de Chile
todos vestimos botas de cowboy
en un sordo diálogo de rock-and-roll.

UNITED STATES

United States
I don't invoke your name
in vain
nor do I denounce you for
deflowering so many stars
I am attached only to your immense solitudes
and I understand it is not your fault
if you invented life
ready-made
not even the golden yesternights
of Miss Monroe.
But admit it,
you had the tragic sickness
of tame peoples
and climbed up the Andean Way
to fill yourself with copper, chromosomes, guns.
Yet thinking it over very carefully
now as I walk through Managua, San Salvador
down Providence Avenue in Santiago de Chile,
we are all wearing cowboy boots
amid a deafening dialog of rock-and-roll.

BALADA DEL DESTERRADO

Apiádate verdugo del exiliado,
del vanamente perseguido
que sólo quiere ver el paisaje
de su tierra
la cordillera de los andes silbándole desde cerca.
los vientos de un vuelo en ascensor
la cabellera enlunada
de la madre
paseándose menuda, inclinada
liviana entre las harinas...

Que regrese señor el errante
el ajeno a toda hora
para que descienda fresco, saltarín por los ríos de la patria
por los bosques tan azules
hasta encontrarse con los tobillos
de la María
y las araucarias de la memoria.

Escucha señor
que no te arrepentirás
del silencio del forastero
que ante el tiempo degollado
ensordece y espera entrecortado.

Déjalo señor
que regrese al patio de su casa
a la paz de las gallinas
a los limoneros en sus sitios
a las basuras de su calle
al rostro de un día
en su país.

THE EXILE'S BALLAD

Have pity señor Hangman
on the exile,
the one hunted for no reason
who only wants to see the landscape
of his earth
close by the cordillera of the Andes whistling to him
the winds of ascending wings
the moonlit hair
of the mother
walking back and forth small, bent
slight between the flour and the salt.

Señor, let return the wanderer
the stranger every hour of the day
so that he may go leapfrogging, frisky
down the rivers of the fatherland
through intense blue groves
until he runs into Maria's heels
and the remembered araucaria flowers.

Listen señor
you will not regret the silence of the outsider
who in cutthroat times
grows deaf and waits broken.

Señor, let him return
to the patio of his house
to the tranquility of the chickens
to the lemon groves
to the garbage in the streets
to the countenance of a day
in his land.

C.F.

MI PAÍS

Mi país
es el aire tan
nuestro
en las noches fugitivas
de Atitlán.

Es tu rostro
vendado,
aunque salvajemente
hermoso
a pesar de esos
movimientos
entorpecidos
por las ajenas cuchillas
afiebradas.

Y tú
despojada
abierta
herida
eres
iluminada
un faro en los mares del sur.

Mi país
son los gemidos
del hambre,
en la africana noche atrevida
suplicante para que no la olvides.

Como mujer no tengo país
tan sólo piedras y ríos, una ilusión
sin citadelas.

MY COUNTRY

My country
is the air so
much our own
in the fugitive nights
of Atitlán.

It's your blindfolded
face,
still savagely
beautiful
despite those movements
hampered
by the
strange and fevered
knives.

And you
ravaged
open wounded
are aglow
a lighthouse in
the southern seas.

My country is
the moans
of hunger
in the African night, boldly
imploring you not to forget her.

As a woman I have no country
only stones and rivers, an illusion
without citadels.

                                        N.L.

EXTRANJERA

La extranjera
pide un trago
de agua,
un trozo de tierra.
Flotando en la intemperie
de su destierro
el agua la acerca
a la vida de su mundo inventado
y conjura una isla pequeñísima
haciendo un mapa,
geografías,
tatuajes de sus
dolores.

ALIEN

The foreign woman
asks for a drink
of water,
a bit of earth.
Floating, exposed to the elements
of her exile,
water brings her close
to the life of her imaginary world,
and she conjures a tiny island,
making a map,
geographies,
tattoos of her
sorrows.

DEMENCIAS

Trastornada
junto a brumosas letanías, ella
arma viajes,
destapa pertenencias:
aquel cofre de hojas secas
semejantes a las celebraciones falsas
la manta magenta,
traída de los mares de Odesa,
dos o tres fotografías
para acariciar
para cercarlas al cuerpo roto
de cicatrices destempladas.

Y así escondiendo en diluidos paquetes
las efímeras historias,
mientras las botas doradas del terror,
se acercan anunciando
la hora de la muerte,
la hora de los tiempos de la ira
manca,
ella deja atrás
al mar negro
de sus vivencias
se hunde.
Todo es agua.
Salvaje.
Viva.

MADNESS

Deranged,
with misty litanies she
constructs voyages,
uncorks belongings:
that chest of dry leaves resembling a mock celebration,
the magenta blanket brought from the seas of Odessa,
two or three photographs
to caress,
to bring close to the broken body
with its untimely scars.

And thus, concealing the ephemeral
stories in flimsy packages
while the gilded boots of terror
approach, announcing
the hour of her death,
the hour of angry
maimed times,
she leaves behind
the black sea
of understanding,
sinks.
Everything is water.
Wild.
Alive.

UN MUJER DUERME EN UNA ISLA

Una mujer duerme en una isla
y del cabello nacen las moradas
de memorias y pájaros salvajes.
Su cuerpo es un mascarón de proa
y dicen que desde
que durmió en la isla
pareciera haber sido tocada por la lluvias
de la demencia, que su pelo florece en los atardeceres
junto a la música del mar. Otros dicen
que sus párpados dibujan mapas de extrañas geografías,
tatuajes salvajes que ella guarda sólo
en la redondez tenue del sueño.

Una mujer duerme en una isla
y deja de ser ella misma
libre ahora de la tierra.
Navega y bebe
la inmensidad del mar.
Las semillas llenan su pelo que flota
y ella es una isla
rodeada de estrellas.

A WOMAN SLEEPS ON AN ISLAND

A woman sleeps on an island
and from her hair is born the dwelling place
of memories and wild birds.
Her body is a figurehead,
and they say that since
she fell asleep on the island
she seems to have been touched by the rains
of madness, that her hair blossoms each evening
next to the music of the sea. Others say
her eyelids trace maps of strange geographies,
savage tattoos kept only in the tenuous
circle of her dreams.

A woman sleeps on an island
and stops being herself,
free now of the land.
She sails and drinks
the vastness of the sea.
Seeds fill her floating hair;
she is an island
surrounded by stars.

C.F.

REGRESOS

¿Habré dejado las ventanas cerradas?
Los inviernos lluviosos crepitan por las balaustradas
no recuerdo si apagué el brasero
si pude cerrar las cortinas antes de la oscuridad
o de la huida.
¿Alguien habrá barrido el comienzo del otoño
en mi calle?
¿Y la puerta permanecerá abierta para el retorno?

RETURNS

Did I close the windows?
The rainy winters creak down the banisters,
and I can't remember if I put out the fire
or if I closed the curtains before the darkness
or the flight.
Will someone have swept away the beginning of autumn from my street?
And will the door still be open for my return?

R.S.

UMBRALES

I.

En la soledad de una planicie,
los sin patria
caminan adormecidos en busca de puertas,
umbrales como suaves cobijas,
una cama de hojas adormecidas,
una alfombra para contemplar
el delirio
encendido de otoño y sus brumas como sedas.

II.

En el tiempo del bronceado,
de las cúpulas bermejas
yo instalo mi caballete
en el principio del camino,
pinto como si las mismas hojas y el ámbar
fueran mis manos desdobladas,
en el mismo aire perfumado,
entre los tiempos del jazmín y los tigres,
una hoja cae con sus escamas anaranjadas
me toma de la mano.

THRESHOLDS

I.

In the solitude of the plains
those without a homeland
sleepwalk
seeking doorways,
thresholds like soft quilts,
a bed of sleeping leaves,
a rug on which to contemplate
the delirious
blaze of autumn and its silky fogs.

II.

In the bronze and gold season
of autumn haystacks,
I set up my easel
where the road begins.
I paint as though the very leaves and the amber
were my unfolded hands,
in the same perfumed air,
between the seasons of the jasmine and of the tigers
a leaf falls with its orange veins
it takes me by the hand
I am a painter who walks.

M.B.

LA EXTRANJERA

Buscarás otro
paisaje
para hablar con
tus muertos.
Ninguna palabra
responderá a las voces
de tus amores.
Inventarás otra mirada
y te desplazarás cabizbaja como herida
tras las ciudades prestadas.

Sabrás que
ya no habrá para ti ningún regreso
y nombrarás a los que hicieron
de tu memoria
un lenguaje de huerfanías.
Pensarás en otros alientos
porque eres lejana y sola
porque tu lengua
lleva la sombra de los extraños.

THE FOREIGNER

You will search for another
landscape in which
to speak with
your dead.
No words
will respond to the voices of your love.
You will make up another gaze
and you will walk with your head bowed as if wounded
in borrowed cities.

You will know that there will be no return for you
and you will name those who made
of your memory
a language of orphanhood.
You will think of other breaths
because yours are distant and alone
because your language
carries the shadows of strangers.

M.B.G.

SIN REGRESOS

Sin regresos,
sin historias ni origen,
ella es extraña, ajena.
Las fotografías de sus padres,
no son las de sus padres.
Tal vez, son los padres de otros extraños.
Ella se ha quedado sola
en el espacio de las paredes
blancas,
en un silencio rajado.
Camina hacia el desierto
erguida, distante,
hacia los espejismos de las ciudades
nuevas.

WITHOUT BACKTRACKING

Without backtracking,
without histories or origin
she is a stranger, absent.
The photographs of her parents,
are not those of her parents.
Perhaps, they're the parents of other strangers.
She has remained alone
between the white
walls,
in a cracked silence.
She walks toward the desert
erect, distant,
toward the mirages of new
cities.

LOS EMIGRANTES

I.

Fuimos hábiles
en preparar la huida,
frágiles en nuestras
pertenencias
Mamá trajo pedazos de tierra fresca
piedras para recordar a los
muertos que dejábamos
una que otra fotografía
suspendida en la dispersión
de nuestras geneologías
un candelabro de siete velas
para alumbrar la oscuridad
de los emigrantes.

II.

Nos fuimos
con pasos alados
repitiendo la historia de ellos
ahora, nosotros
nos recibieron
como se reciben a los
extranjeros
con parca cortesía
con sutiles sospechas

III.

Aprendimos a vivir entre lo ajeno
a soñar con las buganvillas
el balcón de la casa junto al mar
ningún cuaderno de la memoria
amenguó esas tristezas, como pozos oscuros
vivimos
con nuestras manos

EMIGRANTS

I.

We were clever
in preparing for the flight
fragile in our
possessions
Mother brought along pieces of fresh earth
stones to remember the
dead we left behind
a few photographs
suspended in the dispersion
of our genealogies
a candelabrum of seven candles
to illuminate the darkness
of emigrants.

II.

We left
with winged steps
repeating the history of others
now, us
they received us
like foreigners are
received
with moderate courtesy
subtle suspicions.

III.

We learned to live among foreign things
to dream about bougainvillea
the balcony of the house by the sea
no scrapbook of memory
diminished those sorrows, like dark wells
we lived
with our hands

extendidas a la posibilidad del
horizonte
al agua, al cielo que no era nuestro,
sin preguntas ni respuestas
tal vez éramos
esa fotografía en sepia
suspendida en un calendario
sin horas ni estaciones
errando por ciudades inhóspitas
buscando hospedajes
en los jardines del invierno.

IV.

Los emigrantes
cruzando intrépidas fronteras
imaginando gestos de ausencia en
la lejanía
hoy después del día extendido
en la tierras de hielo oscuro
aprenden otro modo de ser
en otra lengua
repiten las correctas preposiciones
la dimensión del odio y la mesura
aprenden de la prisa
y del desencanto
solos, ajenos
en mesas vacías
la memoria es una sílaba nueva
una voz por hacerse
solos repiten en voz baja
el inglés los hace más fuertes
y diminutas en sus nostalgias
perdidos, sueñan con la raíz del otoño
las hojas vacilantes
la fragilidad de las huidas.

extended toward the possibility of a
horizon
to the water and sky that weren't ours
without questions or answers
perhaps we were
that photograph in sepia
suspended on a calendar
without hours or seasons
wandering through inhospitable cities
looking for lodging
in winter gardens.

IV.

Emigrants
crossing intrepid borders
imagining gestures of absence in
the distance
today, after a long time and
in ice-darkened lands
they learn another way of being
in another language
they repeat correct prepositions
the dimension of hatred and civility
they learn in haste
and in disillusionment
alone, foreign
at empty tables
memory is a new syllable
a voice to be made
alone they repeat softly
English makes them stronger
and small in their nostalgia
lost, they dream about the beginning of autumn
the changing leaves
the fragility of flights.

C.K.C.

THE DISPOSSESSED

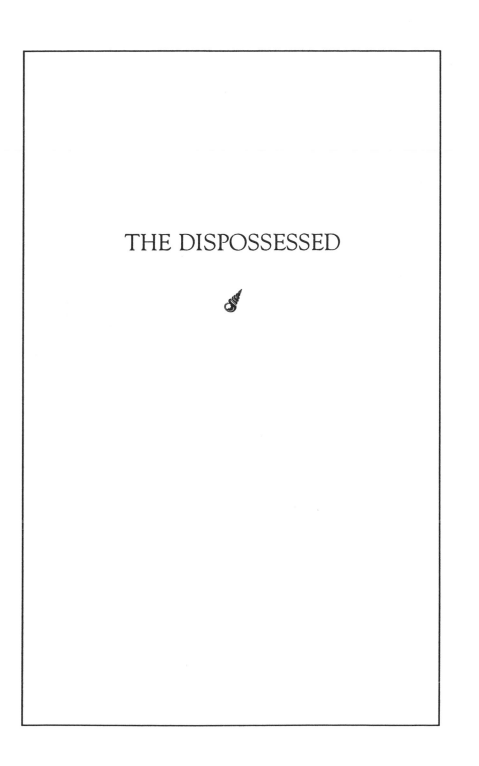

LA INDOCUMENTADA

Indocumentada
con los alfabetos vacíos
y un abanico de huesos
girando entre los dedos
he olvidado las palabras
que nunca existieron
porque ellos me nombraban
al penetrarme en una
redondez de nubes
y secretos consagrados.

Indocumentada soy
la mujer
sin consonantes ni sonidos
sin mi nombre
para pronunciarme
y mis cabellos
son granizos, neblina
tiemblan
al escribirme
al juntar alimentos
porque todos
me echan de
los clubes
de los cines
de la sociedad de escritores
y los viejos poetas
hacen suyos mis
decires
mientras me llaman
angel, pez, luz
y puta
por supuesto
mujer.

WOMAN WITHOUT PAPERS

Woman without papers
with alphabets missing
and a fan of bones
whirling between the fingers
I have forgotten the words
that never existed
because they named me as they entered me
in a roundness of clouds
and sacred secrets.

Without papers I am
the woman
with neither consonants nor sounds
with no name
to pronounce myself
and my hair
is hail, fog
that trembles
as I inscribe myself
as I gather up food
because they all
throw me out
of the clubs
of the movies
and society of writers
and the old poets
take for their own my
sayings
while calling me
angel, fish, light
and whore
woman
of course.

LA MESA DE BILLAR EN NEW BEDFORD, MASS.

Ella entró vestida
era clara y encorvada como un día cualquiera
o como un otro día,
ella era redonda y joven
con algo de Eva y con algo de María.
Pero, ellos le vieron desnuda,
entraron bruscos por su pelo largo,
su pelo como cenizas
ellos la habitaban por las rendijas de sus ojos que
se nublaban
mientras los falos asustados
la despedazaban como un trapo malgastado entre
las cacerolas.

Ella entró vestida
como una luna
y le fueron deshojando sus misterios
sus faldas que se mecían
entre los dientes de los enanos rompiéndola, escupiéndola,
acariciándola,
vagamente, torpemente.

Ella era celeste y vestía colores de río,
y ahora coagulada fermentada, deforme
un una mesa de billar
New Bedford, Massachusetts
pueblo de ballenas y algunos hombres malolientes.

En la mesa de billar,
ella flotaba eternamente abierta despojada de claridades
y ellos hurgueteaban su vagina que ahora humeaba como una cloaca
como una boca de ballena naúfraga
incendiada entre los despojos.

THE BILLIARD TABLE IN NEW BEDFORD, MA

She came in clothed,
she was radiant and shaped like an ordinary day
or like another day,
she was soft, young,
with something of Eve and something of Mary.
But they saw her as naked
they stormed her long hair
her hair pale as ashes
burst through the crevices of her eyes that
grew dim
as the shocked phalluses
tore her to pieces like a worn-out rag among
the pots and pans.

She came in clothed
like a moon
and they kept stripping away her mysteries
her skirts that were dangling
between the teeth of the dwarves splitting her, spitting her out,
fondling her
vaguely, crudely.

She was sky-like and wearing river colors
and now clotted, fermented, deformed,
on a billiard table
New Bedford, Massachusetts
town of whales and some foul-smelling men.

On the billiard table,
she was floating eternally open stripped of all brightness
and they were smearing her vagina, now fuming like a sewer
like the mouth of a drowned whale
blazing amid the refuse.

Su blusa
era una ráfaga de humo chamusqueada
y ellos no la veían
ya no la veían desnuda
porque era una enrollada presa de colores purpúreos en
una mesa de billar
sus brazos inutilizados
no podrían colgarse del que tal vez la quiso
y ahora como una carne en una carnicería de velorios,
      amarrada a la mesa de billar

Ella duerme desnuda.

Her blouse
was a searing whirlwind of smoke
and they didn't see her
now they didn't see her naked
because she had become a purple huddle of plunder on
a billiard table
her arms made useless
could no longer embrace the one who once perhaps loved her
and now like a piece of meat being mourned in a slaughterhouse,
      bound to the billiard table.

She sleeps naked.

C.F.

SALEM

En la jadeante y triste
luz de Salem,
junto a las ramas que arden
como emblemas nefastos,
en ese encorvado año
de la hora oculta: 1692.
Devoraron las entrañas
de mi mantilla fosforescente,
verde como los sueños de
Irlanda.

Me rajaron
en una torre
mi cabellera indomable.
bondadosa.

El más pérfido
cortó mis orejas
y los sonidos del
agua le apagaron
la sed de sus manos mancas.

Me acusaron de envenenar
tortas, dulces, pasteles,
cuando yo jamás fui
cocinera,
sólo acumulaba hierbas para
sanar alegrías y espasmos.

Fui cristalizada
con mis manuscritos y conjuros
mis débiles posesiones,
el candelabro
de mi abuela.

SALEM

In the sad and gasping
light of Salem,
where branches burn
like signs of things turned bad,
in this huddled year
of the hidden time: 1692.
They left it gutted,
my phosphorescent shawl,
green as dreams of
Ireland.

In a tower,
they left me shorn
of my stubborn
goodhearted hair.

The lowest of them all
cut off my ears
and the sounds of
water slaked
the thirst in his wanting hands

They claimed I poisoned
pastries, cakes, and sweets,
but I was never
any cook,
I only gathered herbs to
soothe commotions of the fits.

I was crystallized
with my manuscripts and spells
my frail belongings,
my grandma's
candle-tree.   N.L.

DESNUDAS EN LOS BOSQUES DE ALAMBRE

I.

A veces me disfrazaba de sacerdotiza, dando saltos por el aire.
A veces visitábamos prostíbulos y lavábamos sus paredes con hojas
    de rosa cobriza.
A veces jugamos a mirarnos, a ver las olas en la brisa.
La verdad era incierta. Las sirenas de las alarmas estables, seguras.
Entonces tú y yo nos queríamos con una especie de perversa y
censurada locura. Gozaba en desnudarte, enredarte en una bufanda de
lana picante, morder las diminutas y sinceras uñas, llenar tu espalda
de miel, dejar que las estaciones, los osos, limpien las desjuiciadas
heridas del amor.
—Tú esperabas el momento preciso para cortar mi cabello de princesa
rusa;
teñirlo de algas venenosas que conservabas a la orilla de tus pies. A
veces, me golpeabas las manos, ceremonioso, como un anciano
languideciendo. Yo desmayada fingía soñar en tus cabellos y tú
entrabas desfrenado por las líneas de mis palmas.
Como un mago seguro, espléndido en las caricias, decías: No te
salvarás hasta que nos desnudemos y exploremos las manchas oscuras
del cielo razo.

II.

Nos queríamos entre los indicios y los gestos, entre las uvas de la
medianoche y las ropas amontonadas en esa casa deshabitada. Dudosos
entre las palabras nos llamábamos en secreto con frenesí de delicada
pornografía. Dejó de ser todo. Todas las promesas entre las orejas y
las señales abiertas de los labios cuando me dijiste: Desnúdate judía
ya ahora, rápido, ya desnúdate, ya tendrás plata para hacerte
el remedio.

NAKED GIRLS IN THE FORESTS OF BARBED WIRE

I.

At times I dressed up as a priestess, and went leaping through air.
At times we visited houses of prostitution and washed the walls
     with coppery leaves.
At times we played games of staring at one another, of seeing waves in
the breezes.
Truth was uncertain. The sirens of the alarms stable, secure. Then
you and I loved each other with a kind of perverse and censorious
madness. I loved to take off your clothes, wrap you in a prickly
woolen shawl, nibble your tiny and sincere nails, spread honey over
your shoulder and let the seasons, the bears clean the unthinking
wounds of love.
—You waited for the precise moment to shear my hair of a Russian
princess;
to stain it with the venomous seaweed you always kept at the shore of
your feet. At times you would slap my hands ceremoniously like a
courtly old gentleman. I, trancelike, would pretend to sleep in your
hair, and you would burst wantonly through the lines of my palms.
Like a confident sorcerer, splendid in caresses, you said: You can't
escape until we take off our clothes and explore all the dark
splotches of the ceiling.

II.

We loved each other with signs and gestures, amid grapes at midnight
and piled clothes in that uninhabited house. Not trusting words, we
called out to each other covertly, in a frenzy of delicate
pornography. Suddenly it all ceased to be. All the promises between
the ears and the clear language of the lips when you said to me: Strip
naked Jew girl right now, quick, strip naked hurry, you'll be taken
care of if anything happens.

III.

En la ilusoria tibieza del cuarto, entre los girasoles y las mantas de
lana, sobre las sábanas envestidas de mareas, llegaron por las
murallas, asediaron los inmensos espacios, se alzaron por el volcán de
leños, las desnudas judías de los bosques espesos
en Dachau, Treblinka, Baden-Baden, las desválidas
judías en la neblina humeante.
Desveladas por un bosque de arios reptiles olfateando los pechos, las
nalgas. El cuerpo de una judía destilada por los bosques de alambre.

IV.

Judías desnudas,
indefinidas, en silencio
judías dando gritos de fe a hurtadillas, cerrando piernas, labios con
la dignidad milenaria de los ilusos, estatuas de humo apresuradas hacia
las duchas de gas azul, duchas oscuras
con sabor a viñedos enfermizos.

V.

Judías desnudas
sobrevivientes, desaparecidas gravitando entre tus rodillas, regresando
por el bosque de los alambres. Retornando al cuarto de los hallazgos
demenciales, plasmado de ratas crepitando en una hoguera, bañada en
la muerte oscura, precisa. Tú pareces que crepitas en ese fuego, mientras
los verdugos se cubren de premeditadas sonrisas para observar
un cuerpo esencial; una desnuda mujer judía, dormida con un tatuaje
entre sus piernas.

VI.

Era cierto que tal vez nunca nos supimos mirar.

III.
Streaming into the illusory warmth of the room they come, drift among
the sunflowers and the woolen covers, hover over sheets blessed with
sea breezes, invade through the walls, besiege the immense space,
erupt through the volcano of tree trunks, the naked Jewish girls from
the thick forests of Dachau, Treblinka, Baden-Baden, defenseless
Jewish girls coming through the smoky fog. Defenseless before a
forest of Aryan serpents slithering over breasts, buttocks. The body
of one Jewish girl distilled from the forests of barbed wire.

IV.
Naked Jewish girls
nameless, silent
Jewish girls contriving to call out words of faith, closing legs and lips
with the ancient dignity of the innocent,
statues of smoke hurried into showers of blue gas, black showers
with the taste of sickly vineyards.

V.
Naked Jewish girls
the survivors, the vanished ones sinking down heavily between your
knees, come back from the forests of barbed wire. Come back to the
place of demented discoveries, machination of rats, crackling
bonfire, bathed in death, black, exact. You too seem to crackle in
that fire, while the hangmen premeditated smiles on their faces the
better to see an elemental body: a naked Jewish woman asleep, tattoo
between the legs.

VI.
Clear that never had we known how to see ourselves.

C.F.

LO QUE ERA YUGOSLAVIA

I.

Vacíos, desprendiéndose,
con lo que fue una mirada victoriosa
ahí están pidiendo un instante más,
un aliento más
para acariciar
las murallas de
Dubrovnik
o tan sólo mojarse el corazón
en la ciudad de los buenos.

II.

¿Dónde estabas tú cuando llegaron a
tus umbrales los niños de la guerra?
¿Con qué agua viva los
hiciste renacer?
¿Con qué poemas hablaste
de ellos?
¿Con qué lengua los llamaste?

III.

En Dubrovnik
derribados los cuerpos
de los niños
semejantes a frágiles deslavados
ángeles sumidos siempre en claridades.

IV.

Ahí
están detenidos
en una funesta
inmobilidad,
y son los niños de la guerra
violentos acabados de silencio.

WHAT WAS YUGOSLAVIA

I.
Empty, dispossessed,
with what was a triumphal look,
here they are asking for one more moment,
one more breath
to embrace
Dubrovnik's
walls
or just to soak their hearts
in this city of good people.

II.
Where were you when the children of war
arrived at your thresholds?
With what life-giving water
did you revive them?
With what poems did you speak
of them?
In what language did you call to them?

III.
In Dubrovnik
the fallen bodies
of children
resemble fragile, unwashed
angels sunk forever in the light.

IV.
Here,
detained
in an ill-fated
immobility,
the children of war
are violent silent endings.

Invisibles ante la cólera
son ellos los niños
cadáveres de la guerra.

V.

En Dubrovnik,
en Belgrado,
en Sarajevo,
yo les digo que los he visto.
Atraviesan el camposanto
con velos rojos de amor sangrante
muertos con navajas de fantasmas malsanos.
Son los ángeles difuntos
y ahí
en Belgrado,
en Sarajevo,
todo se tiñe con el color ocre
de los enfermos
como la memoria de los sonidos agrios
de la guerra.

VI.

Alguien
se escurre.
Entre las piedras
y el silencio de las piedras,
veo a dos que se aman
se pierden en un beso
victorioso,
pero son todavía ángeles difuntos.
Se toman de los rostros
porque alguien les rajó
las piernas
y sin embargo
no han perdido la posibilidad
del asombro.

Their corpses,
invisible
before rage.

V.

In Dubrovnik,
in Belgrade
in Sarajevo,
I tell you I have seen the dead
crossing the cemetery
with red veils of bleeding love,
with jackknives of deathly ghosts.
They are dead angels,
and here
in Belgrade,
in Sarajevo,
everything is tinged a
sickly ocher
like the memory of war's piercing
sharp sounds.

VI.

Someone
scurries off.
Among the stones,
in the silence of the stones,
I watch two lovers
losing themselves in a
triumph's kiss,
but even they are dead angels.
They offer each other their faces
because someone has lacerated
their legs,
and yet
they still haven't lost the ability to feel
life's wonder.

Arqueados se besan
mientras las paredes de Dubrovnik
son sólo la imaginación de la historia,
leyendas raptadas
en las noches del amor sangrante.

Arching, they kiss
while Dubrovnik's walls
exist but in history's imagination,
legends carried off
on nights of bleeding love.

¿Hubiera sido posible acercarse a recoger judíos,
a las escuálidas gitanas?
¿Era posible decirles en el oído calcinado
que aún en la desdoblada Amsterdam,
alguien los amaba,
los escondía de la muerte tibia?
¿No era posible recoger a los inválidos
que esperaban los trenes de la desgracia?
¿Era posible acercarse con la voz
a los niños judíos desvalidos?
¿Era posible ser humano?
Aunque sí era posible
acusar;
denunciar;
prohibir;
espantar a los inválidos;
destruirles las tiendas,
quebrarlos con los cristales del humo empañado.
Era posible
obligarles a desnudarse
con el vaticinio de una estrella tatuada
entre los brazos.

Would it have been possible to take in the Jews,
the squalid gypsies?
Was it possible to whisper in their blackened ears
that even in Amsterdam torn asunder
someone loved them,
would rescue them from the chill of death?
Wasn't it possible to take in all the sick
who were waiting for misfortune's trains?
Was it possible to approach with an open heart
the destitute Jewish children?
Was it possible to be human?
Though, yes, it was possible
to accuse,
to denounce,
to banish,
to terrorize the sick, the crippled,
to destroy shops,
smashing windows, fire-bombing.
It was possible
to force them to undress,
with the prophecy of a Star tattooed
on their breasts.

                                        R.S.

NOCHE

I.

Más allá de la noche,
entre los umbrales cristalinos del sueño,
ellas las viajeras
caminantes con pies de ríos,
viajeras por los pozos errados de la muerte,
buscan, preguntan,
cantan, sollozan
les preguntan a los rosarios
por los días del retorno,
regresan en el secreto sueño de la noche
a la casa de la noche,
a la casa sin palabras,
a las camas pobladas de los muertos
y sus guirnaldas de violetas.

II.

Más allá del día,
se preparan las viajeras,
buscan, preguntan, sollozan.
En el pueblo, todos las conocen
pero les huyen
y ellas insisten en esa dulce tranquila pregunta:
¿Ha visto a mi hijo?

III.

Buscan, cantan, sollozan
les preguntan a los rosarios
a las brujas de las comarcas,
que ofrecen hierbas para el olvido,
y regresan a la casa secreta de la noche,
a la cama poblada de muertos,
a la casa sin lengua,
al idioma austero de la ausencia.

NIGHT

I.

Beyond the night,
among the crystalline thresholds of dream,
the women travelers
with feet sprouting rivers
wanderers through the erroneous wells of death,
search, inquire,
sing, weep
and ask the rosaries
about the day of the homecoming,
return in the secret dream of night
to the pitch-black house,
to the house without words,
to the beds populated by the dead
and their violet garlands.

II.

Beyond the day,
the women travelers prepare themselves,
search inquire and weep.
In the town, everyone knows them
but runs away
and they insist upon that sweet, peaceful question;
Have you seen my son?

III.

They search, sing, weep
and ask the rosaries
and the witches of the district,
who offer herbs for forgetting,
and return to the secret pitch-black house,
to the bed populated by the dead,
to the home without a voice,
to the austere language of absence.

EL MIEDO

El miedo
anidaba
como un murmullo
extraviado en las
gargantas secas.
Nada decíamos,
éramos un arpa carcomida,
pequeños gemidos
en la proximidad
de todas estas perversas
distancias.

A LO LEJOS EL VIENTO

I.

A lo lejos el viento;
a lo lejos el silencio.
Ella se inclina sobre las arenas.
A los lejos alguien ilumina las
ciudades lejanas.
Los hombres habitan en su silencio
de extraños.

II.

Ella piensa en los que huyeron,
en los que desamparados tocaron las puertas
de las ciudades
que nadie abría.
Ella piensa en los mendigos
y por eso se sabe segura aquí
en la inmensa vastedad
de todos los desiertos.

FEAR

Fear
nested
like a murmur
lost in
parched throats.
We said nothing,
we were like decayed harps,
little moans
in the proximity
of all these perverse
distances.

DISTANT WIND

I.

In the distance, wind;
in the distance, silence.
She leans over the sand.
In the distance someone illuminates
far-off cities.
Men reside in their silence
of strangers.

II.

She thinks of those who fled,
of the abandoned ones who called
at the city doors
that no one opened.
She things of the beggars
and this is why she feels
secure here in the immense vastness
of all the deserts.

EL PALACIO DE LOS GOBERNADORES, SANTA FE

En el palacio de los
gobernadores donde la Historia
erró sus travesías
condenando la verdad sencilla,
ellos, los derrotados,
murmuran.
Tan sólo se reconocen
ante el doblegado dolor
de tiempos y tierras truncadas,
de una dignidad usurpada.

Los turistas cada vez más blancos
asustadizos ante el sol provocante
regatean por el precio de las turquesas
sangrantes
no cesan en sus exigencias.
Después de todo,
son los indios cochinos
los que venden sus mercancías.

Ellos, adormecidos
con el cuerpo llagado
se inclinan ante sus cestas de ángeles
pulen las piedras hablantes
errando la historia
regalan sus obsequios
sus secretos y sus manos como alas.

En el palacio de los gobernadores
cuando la tarde es un tajo violeta
los ex-dueños de esta América
se marchan a las aldeas pedregosas
en vehículos de mala muerte;
adormecidos ya no reconocen a la tierra

THE PALACE OF GOVERNORS, SANTA FE

In the governors'
palace
where History
missed its crossroads
condemning simple truth,
they, the vanquished,
murmur.
They only recognize one another
before the redoubled sorrow
of truncated lands and times
of usurped dignity.

The tourists, each time whiter,
frightened before the provoking sun
haggle over the price of bleeding
turquoise
unceasing in their demands.
After all,
these are the filthy Indians
selling their goods.

Drowsy,
with injured bodies
they lean on their angelic baskets,
polish the talking stones lost in history
giving away their gifts,
their secrets and their hands like wings.

In the governors' palace
when the afternoon is a slice of violet,
the former landlords of America
leave for their stony towns
in death-defying vehicles;
sleepy, they no longer recognize the land

ni dónde están
ni el nombre oculto de su idioma.

Por la noche
queda el palacio de los gobernadores
aullando con los ángeles feroces,
con las calaveras remecidas por vientos malos
y el ruido de la noche
es un aullido extranjero
aquí en la ciudad de verano
donde los hombres blancos
duermen tranquilos
olvidando sus masacres.

or where they are
or the hidden names of their language.

During the night
the governors' palace is left behind
howling with ferocious angels,
with skeletons rocked by evil winds
and the noise of the evening
is a foreign cry
here in the summer city
where the white men
sleep peacefully
forgetting their massacres.

C.K.C.

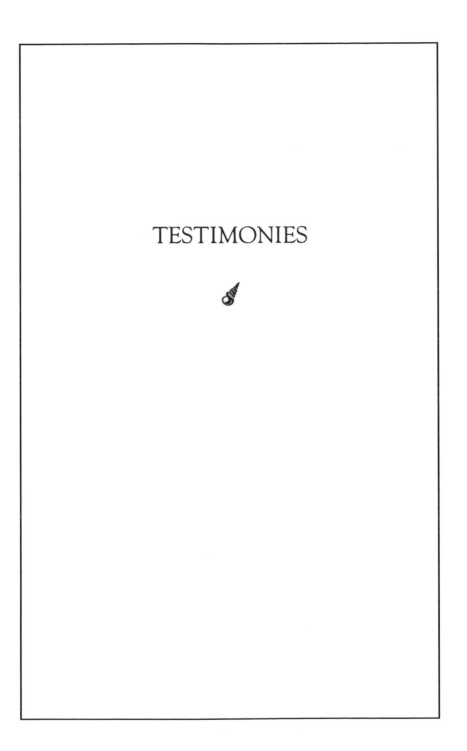

TESTIMONIES

LOS DESAPARECIDOS

Los desaparecidos,
¿Dónde están?
¿Dónde está el Miguel con el pan en los bolsillos?
¿Dónde está la señora Rosa?
y el eco de la sangre
empaña preguntas,
y el aire se me mancha como la sangre.

Una rajadura,
una costra como un grito en el sepulcro,
vaticinan que las gargantas segregan silencios,
palabras nunca y siempre dichas
despedidas del amanecer y el amor.

Yo soy hembra sin fusil
pequeña y de cabellos azules como el ácido
que busca tras los hospitales de una morgue improvisada
tras iglesias censuradas
tras los signos de mis viudas
entonces
yo juro apoderarme de la palabra
ir con ella por los muros de la ciudad
ir con ella donde anduvo el látigo
ir con esta palabra
que Dios no me dió
al encuentro de las bocas desdentadas
como el hambre
ir en busca de tus ojos.

Yo juro ser la palabra
pero nunca lamentar a los
muertos que hoy y siempre
están.

THE DISAPPEARED ONES

The disappeared ones,
Where are they now?
Where is Miguel with his pockets full of bread?
Where is Señora Rosa?
and the echo of blood
muffles questions
and the air itself splatters me with blood.

A split,
a scab like a scream in the grave
foretell throats spilling silences
words never and always said
farewells to dawn and to love.

I am an unarmed woman
small and with hair blue as acid.
I search behind hospitals for a makeshift morgue
behind forbidden churches
beneath the traces of my Chilean widows
then
I swear to arm myself with the word
take it along the walls of the city
take it where the whip went
take this word
not given by God
to seek out the toothless mouths
as hunger does
go in search of your eyes.

I swear to be the word
but never to lament the dead
who are present.
Now.
Forever.

LO MÁS INCREÍBLE

Lo más increíble
eran gente como nosotros
bien educados y finos.
Versados en las ciencias abstractas,
asistían al palco de las sinfonías
al dentista
a las escuelitas privadas
algunos jugaban al golf...

Sí, gente como usted, como yo
padres de familia
abuelos
tíos y compadres.

Pero enloquecieron
se deleitaban en las quemas
de niños y libros,
jugaban a decorar cementerios
compraban muebles de huesos mancos
comían orejitas y testículos.

Se figuraban ser invencibles
ceremoniosos ante el deber
y hablaban de la tortura
con palabras de médicos y carniceros.

Asesinaron a los jóvenes de mi país
y del tuyo.
Ya nadie podría creer en Alicia tras los espejos
ya nadie podría pasearse por las avenidas
sin el terror calándose entre los huesos.

THE MOST UNBELIEVABLE PART

The most unbelievable part,
they were people like us
good manners
well-educated and refined.
Versed in abstract sciences,
always took a box for the symphony
made regular trips to the dentist
attended very nice prep schools
some played golf.

Yes, people like you, like me
family men
grandfathers
uncles and godfathers.

But they went crazy
delighted in burning
children and books
played at decorating cemeteries
bought furniture made of broken bones
dined on tender ears and testicles.

Thought they were invincible
meticulous in their duties
and spoke of torture
in the language of surgeons and butchers.

They assassinated the young of my country
and of yours.
now nobody could believe in Alice through the looking glass,
now nobody could stroll along the avenues
without terror bursting through their bones.

Y lo más increíble
era gente
como usted
como yo
sí, gente fina
como nosotros.

And the most unbelievable part
they were people
like you
like me
yes, nice people
just like us.

ANA FRANK Y NOSOTRAS

I.
Como una cicatriz
atada a las
dolencias de
la noche,
Ana Frank
me visita con frecuencia.

II.
Lleva lazos de ausencias,
a veces, lleva
mirada de lluvia y algas
y sus ojos se posan inquietos dentro
de los míos para que mi mirada
la sobreviva, la cuente
o la haga.

III.
Me pregunta María del Carmen
si conozco a todos mis muertos,
se me acerca diáfana o diabólica,
yo no puedo prometerle regresos,
ni descubrirle su mirada desvelada,
su mirada de dagas e insomnios.

IV.
Sonia de las Mercedes
me visita con frecuencia
mientras como, sueño, amo o bebo
hay un eco de la muerte entre nosotras,
hay un eco de la vida
entre nosotras.

ANNE FRANK AND US

I.
Like a scar
attached to
the aches of
nighttime,
Anne Frank
visits me often.

II.
She comes bringing loops of absences,
at times she brings
a glance of rain and seaweed
and her eyes alight restively upon
my own so that my glance
will survive her, tell her
or be her.

III.
María del Carmen asks me
if I know all my dead,
she comes near me diaphanous or diabolical
and I can't promise her returns
nor can I discern her wakeful glance,
her glance of daggers and sleeplessness.

IV.
Sonia de las Mercedes
often visits me
while I'm eating, dreaming, loving, or drinking
there's an echo of death between us,
there's an echo of life
between us.

V.

Cecilia Gabriela y yo
nos hemos hecho amigas
le cuento de mis sueños, las cenizas y las dichas de las palabras.
Ella me sonríe acusándome piadosamente.
Ella me sonríe para que le devuelva una mirada
para que la mire una y otra vez
muerta bajo los alambres del espanto.
Pero viva en la mirada que la sobrevive.

VI.

María Cecilia me visita.
A tí también te visita.
no podemos transfigurarla ni aniquilarla con
árboles muertos.

Ella es espléndida en su resplandor,
y en sus olores a muerte clausurada.

Ana Frank, María del Carmen, Sonia de las Mercedes,
Cecilia Gabriela, me despiertan en las noches
para pedirme
que no las olvide.

V.

Cecilia Gabriela and I
have become friends
I tell her my dreams, the ashes and happiness of words.
She smiles at me, accusingly, compassionately.
She smiles at me so that I'll return her glance,
keep looking at her again and again
dead beneath the wires of terror.
Alive in the glance that survives her.

VI.

María Cecilia visits me.
She visits you too.
We cannot transfigure her or annihilate her
with dead trees.

She is resplendent in her splendor,
in her aroma of cloistered death.

Anne Frank, María del Carmen, Sonia de las Mercedes,
Cecilia Gabriela, they all wake me up at night
to ask me
not to forget them.

LOS OJOS DE LOS ENTERRADOS

Los ojos de los enterrados,
como en una lejanía inquieta,
nos amenazan
óyelos, óyeme.

El que sobrevive,
en letanías de
memorias prestadas
se estremece, se verifica
porque tan sólo los muertos-moribundos
transfigurados por los sabores del olvido
pueden aparecer,
cautivándonos en esa memoria-mirada que acecha.

Ahí estás Ana Frank,
entre inocente y pérfida
comiéndonos mientras te miramos.
Tú eres los ojos de los enterrados.
Y nos devuelves esa mirada
cadavérica o diabólica.

Ahí estás Milena tan abandonada con la estrella de David cubriéndote
como látigo o promesa.

Ahí estás Lila Valdenegro. Desaparecida. Carnet 353,
olvidada en la memoria que no desmiente.
Los ojos de los enterrados
nos acusan
se acusan,
escribo, me miran
y me atraviesan
las ausencias.

THE EYES OF THE INTERRED

The eyes of the interred,
as in a restless distance,
threaten us
listen to them, listen to me,.

The survivor,
in litanies of borrowed memories
trembles, inspects himself
because only the dead-dying
transfigured by the savors of oblivion
may appear,
capturing us in that backglance-foreglimpse lying in wait.

There you are Anne Frank,
between innocent and devious
devouring us as we look at you.
You are the eyes of the interred.
And you send us back that glance
cadaverous or diabolical.

There you are Milena so abandoned with the Star of David covering you
like a lash or promise.

There you are Lila Valdenegro. Disappeared. I.D. number 353,
forgotten in a memory that does not deny.
The eyes of the interred
accuse us,
accuse themselves,
I write, they watch me
and the absences
transfix me.

C.F.

HERMANA AMADA

I.
Hermana amada,
mujer de cicatrices y solsticios
amiga de los pordioseros
eterna compañera de los torturados
ven, ayúdame en la amanecida.
Déjame poner un sueño en tus faldas
que lavaron el dolor agrio, inundado. de los despellejados.

II.
Déjame morirme
en tus brazos de sol y sangre que se
deshacen para volver a llenarse
de veranos fresas, pieles alegres del Sur.

III.
Amiga mía,
hermana,
amada danzarina de las fuentes,
de los cuerpos que acechan la extensión del amor,
déjame ser palabra en tu ausencia.

IV.
Amada, mientras alzas tus manos
y tus palmas son los senderos,
los ríos, las historias de luces y luciérnagas
madre amada
compañera de planetas, duelos y nacimientos
verde, verdosa dama
déjame ser
tu hija.

BELOVED SISTER

I.

Beloved sister,
woman of scars and solstices
friend of beggars
eternal companion of the tortured
come, help me at the break of dawn.
In your skirts that washed the bitter,
inundated grief of the despoiled,
let me place a dream.

II.

Let me die
in your arms of sunlight and blood that dissolve to fill up again
with summer strawberries and bright southern hides.

III.

My friend,
sister
beloved dancer of the fountains
and of the bodies that wait for love's embrace,
let me be the word in your absence.

IV.

Beloved, as you raise your hands
and your palms become the trails,
the rivers, the stories of light and fireflies,
beloved mother,
companion of planets, tribulations and births,
green, greenish lady
let me be your daughter.

SONIDOS

Las palabras se desgarraron del sonido.
Emigraron feroces en el comienzo de mi labio.
Cosas extrañas se colaban en mi sed,
flores no fecundadas
hervían en mi paladar
amordazado.
Emigré de mí misma,
quise condenarme en el abecedario de las mudas,
para así no gritar,
así no aullar,
para así decir sin el decir.
Las palabras desgarraron la oscuridad de mi tiniebla enmudecida.
Quise ser entonces
la palabra misma de la voz,
repetir un nombre.

SOUNDS

The words broke away from the sound.
They emigrated ferociously to the edge of my lips.
Strange things filtered into my thirst, fruitless
flowers seethed in my
silenced palate.
I emigrated from myself;
I tried to condemn myself to the language of the deaf,
so as not to cry out,
so as not to wail,
so as to tell without telling.
The words tore into the obscurity of my silenced darkness.
Then I tried to be
the spoken word,
so I could repeat a name.

C.K.C.

HORAS DEL TÉ

¿Cómo conversar con un torturador,
estrechar su mano manchada
por las iras y la demencia,
sentarse a su mesa,
hundir mis ojos en los suyos?
¿Preguntarle si se acuerda
del rostro de Miguel,
cómo hacía música con las cadenas?
¿De qué tema hablar
con un torturador?
¿Del alza del café?
¿De la carestía del costo de la vida,
de los años en que las
calles eran una lápida silenciosa
de cuerpos despojados?
¿Cómo conversar con un torturador,
cuyo hijo va al colegio
con el mío?
¿Qué decirle,
mientras mi garganta ensangrentada
pregunta por mi hijo?
¿Ese hijo dorado que
él no recuerda pero sí escucha aullar en las ciudades del miedo,
en las santísimas noches del espanto
en el umbral de su alma encarcelada?

TEA TIME

How to have a conversation with a torturer,
shake his hand soiled
by rage and insanity,
to sit at his table,
bury my eyes in his?
To ask him if he remembers
Miguel's face,
how he made music with his chains?
What to talk about
with a torturer?
The rising price of coffee?
The high cost of living?
The years when the
streets were silent stone slabs
covered with naked, dispossessed bodies?
How to talk with a torturer
whose son goes to school with mine?
What to say
while my blood-filled throat
asks about my son,
that radiant boy
he does not remember
but does hear howling in the cities of fear
on holy nights of terror,
on the threshold of his imprisoned soul?

ELLOS

Se asoman, indolentes,
ataviados con las botas acuchilladas;
se acercan a los cafés
desfilan orgullosos
con abultadas y pequeñísimas insignias:
míralos
no te olvides que son ellos,
no calles,
no temas,
son más pequeñitos aun
sin uniformes
de lata destripada.
Son los perdonados,
los que en nombre de Dios
y la patria
le quitaron los ojos
a tu hijo
lo desnudaron para
humillarlo mejor
en su inocencia de los trece años;
ellos mismos,
los que una y otra vez violaron a tu hija
en las celdas de la demencia,
y ahora pasean por las ciudades
con las manos escondidas.

THEY

There they are, the indolent ones,
wearing their beat-up boots;
they approach the cafés
parade proudly by
showing off their bulging and tiny insignias:
look at them
don't forget who they are
don't keep quiet
don't be afraid
for they are even smaller
without their uniforms,
like guttered animals.
They are the pardoned ones,
those who in the name of God
and country
tore out your son's
eyes
stripped him naked
so as to humiliate him more
in his thirteen-year-old innocence;
they,
those who over and over and over
raped your daughter
in depravity's cells
and now stroll through cities
with their hands hidden.

LAS BICICLETAS

Comenzaron a prohibirte las bicicletas,
a no salir pasadas las ocho,
a sólo comprar en ciertos almacenes
para judíos,
a sólo transitar por ciertas avenidas
a llevar una estrella dorada entre los brazos abiertos,
floridos.
Tus calles se poblaron de sedientos y
miedosos.
Tus pies dejaron de transitar por el aliento
del pasto
y sin embargo,
te gustaba la vida,
las mariposas,
las madrugadas de los que viajan
sin dirección precisa
con la estrella de David iluminándolos.

BICYCLES

It began with the banning of your bicycles,
banning you from going out after eight at night,
restricting you to only buying goods in certain shops
for Jews,
to only walking down certain avenues
with a gold star between your open, blossoming
arms.
Your streets were filled with the thirsty and
fear-stricken.
Your feet quit crossing through windswept
pastures,
and yet
you loved life,
the butterflies,
dawns filled with all those wandering
in no particular direction,
the Star of David illuminating them.

R.S.

DOMINGA

–Para las víctimas de El Mozote y para Claudia Bernardi

Mucho estuve adormecida entre los
escombros.
Los aullidos
de los otros desvirtuaban mis oídos.
Allá, muy cerquita.
allá no más,
yo parecía estar muerta,
entre ellos,
los niños y sus trajecitos del domingo.
Luego me supe viva,
y les cuento más lo que
vi y lo que oí.

Soy Dominga Faustino
del Mozote,
del Salvador.
Mi lengua quedó arropada en el silencio,
apapachada de miedo.
Por muchos días, o tal vez años
no encontré palabras.
Yo también
me había muerto con ellos
y pensé que esto era el cielo;
una tierra muy gruesa y oscura.

Entonces, alguien me despertó.
Eran los ecos de las niñas
muertas
y los árboles se sonrojaron
también con todas esas
risas.
Estoy viva.
Tuve frío.

DOMINGA

— For the victims of El Mozote & for Claudia Bernardi

I was asleep for a long time among
the rubble.
The howls
of the others rang in my ears.
There, very close
just over there,
I seemed to be dead,
among them,
the children and their Sunday outfits.
Then I discovered myself alive,
and I will tell you more
about what I saw and heard.

I am Dominga Faustino
del Mozote,
from Salvador.
My voice remained clothed in silence,
cuddled in fear.
For many days, or maybe years
I did not find the words.
I also
had died with them
and thought that this was heaven;
a very thick and dark clump of soil.

Then, someone woke me.
It was the echoes of the
dead girls
the trees blushed
with all their
laughter.
I am alive.
I was cold.

El miedo era una navaja cóncava.
No llegaron los ángeles
como el cura nos había asegurado.
Pero yo viví.

Les quiero contar que mataron
a los niños, a las mujeres
a las mujeres
con niños adentro.
Se las llevaron más allá del cerro.
Vivas se las llevaron y
de pronto se oían gritos.
Las enormes fogatas en
todos los cerros
llevaban los vestidos
rojizos de la muerte
y de la vida que luchaba.
Los soldados se ponían los zapatos de los
muertos y bailaban con ellos
y se llevaban las joyitas de lata.
Así eran estos jóvenes.
Eran niños del bosque salvaje.
No los vi pero sentí
el replicar de sus salvajes palabras.

Por muchos años no salí de estos árboles.
Parecía que los días eran como
noches
y yo no tenía ni días
ni memoria.
Era mucho antes de los estampidos
y los incendios de la carne mía.
Ahora comienzo a recordar.
El recuerdo es tibio como la sangre,
sangre de sacrificios vacíos.

Fear was a concave knife.
The angels did not arrive
as the priest had assured us.
But I lived.

I want to tell you that they killed
children, women
and women with children inside.
They took them alive beyond the hill.
They took them alive and
suddenly screams were heard.
Enormous bonfires in
all the hills
carried the crimson
dresses of death
and of a life that struggled.
The soldiers put on the shoes of
the dead and danced with them
and took off with the tinsel jewels.
This is how those young men were.
They were children from the wild forest.
I didn't see them but felt
the echoes of their savage words.

For many years I didn't leave these
wooded lands.
The days seemed like
nights
and I didn't have light
or memory.
It was well before the stampedes
and the burning of my flesh.
Now I begin to remember.
Memory is tepid like blood,
the blood of vacant sacrifices.

De pronto,
todo se hizo como un pozo azul de
noche mala.
Alguien llamó a la puerta
y les cortaron la lengua,
como si fuera rosa del jardín.
Yo me arrastré
porque al golpearme me
puse sonámbula, malherida.

Pensaba si todavía
había gente buena por los alrededores
y tan sólo me habían dejado a mi morir
sola o vivir
sola, porque daba
igual eso de ser o no ser,
estar o ser sonámbula sin memoria,
sin otoños claros.
Allí entró el sueño de la muerte
entre los pastizales,
pero me han encontrado
para que les cuente.
He vuelto a amarrar mi telar de sueños
adentro llevo una hija.

Suddenly,
everything became like a blue well in
an evil night.
Someone called at the door
and cut out their tongues,
as if they were garden roses.
I dragged myself
because while beating me,
I became dazed, badly wounded.

I wondered if there were still
good people in the region
and if they simply had left me to die
alone or to live
alone because it was all
the same to be or not to be,
to be or exist dazed, without memory,
without clear autumns.
Death's sleep penetrated there
among the pasture lands,
but they have found me
so that I will tell you.
I have begun to tie up my dream bag
I carry a daughter inside it.

LAS VIUDAS DE CALAMA

Quiero hablarte de ellas.
Las sueño en las orillas
más allá del desfiladero.
Son mujeres ahuecadas,
loceras agrietadas
en un mar sin agua.
Las veo desplazarse solas
como en rumores.

Quiero hablarte de ellas.
Escúchame sin premura.
Son las viudas del desierto.
Son hermanas.
Están como inclinadas, como huidizas
con unas plumas azules, respirando en paz
mientras buscan.
No hay para ellas ni sombras ni olvidos.

Vagan de día, de noche.
Se inclinan cuando el desierto es granate,
cuando el sol alarga y desvirtúa las formas,
pero ahí están
otra vez, buscándolos.
Yo no sé si están muertas o vivas.
Sólo sé que peinan la arena
como si se tratara de los
encajes del amor.

Todo esto yo quiero contarte
para poder decirte a ti lo que veo
esta mañana en el desierto.
Lo que veo en la penumbra cuando
los cerros aullan y los lagartos
adquieren la fosforescencia

THE WIDOWS OF CALAMA

I want to talk to you about them.
I dream about them on the shoreline,
beyond the narrow pass.
They are hollow women,
cracked pieces of clay
in a waterless sea.
I see them move alone
as in whispers.

I want to talk to you about them.
Listen to me without haste.
They are widows of the desert.
Sisters.
They are bent over, as if fleeing
with blue feathers and breathing
peacefully while they search.
There is for them no oblivion or shadows.

They wander day and night,
and bend over when the desert turns to granite,
when the sun stretches and distorts shapes,
but there they are
again, searching for them.
I don't know if they are dead or alive.
I only know they comb the sand
as if it were
lover's lace.

I want to tell you all this
so I can tell you what I see
in the desert this morning.
What I see in the shadows when
the hills howl and lizards
acquire the phosphorescence

de la magia,
del sueño y la vigilia.
Ahí están ellas
te cuento; ahí están,
junto a las cruces oscuras,
junto a los zapatos vacíos que
los llenan de piedras y de flores.

Alguien, de repente,
dice haber encontrado una mano
y todas se acercan sobre
esa arena honda y silenciosa
como desesperadas
para poder apoderarse
de las cosas de la muerte.

Siguen buscando interminables
sin fatiga.
La mano es una pluma.
Igual la aman.

La visten de rojo.
Siguen buscando con
sus manos de plumas,
con esa mano de pluma
que está viva con ojos.

El desierto había preservado ese cuerpo.
Eran muchos los muertos que
habían descansado en estos parajes
y el desierto los escondió.

Las viudas danzaban con una pluma
sobre la muda arena.
Eso hacían las viudas del desierto.
Hacían flores de papel

of magic,
dream and vigilance.
There they are
I tell you; there they are,
next to the dark crosses,
next to the empty shoes that
they fill with rocks and flowers.

Someone, suddenly,
says she has found a hand
and they all gather over that
deep and silent sand
like mad women
trying to overcome
the things of death.

They continue searching endlessly
without fatigue.
The hand is a feather.
They love it equally.

They dress it in red.
They continue searching with
their hands like feathers,
with that feathered hand
that is alive with eyes.

The desert had preserved that body.
Many were the dead that
had rested in these places
and the desert concealed them.

The widows danced with a feather
on the silent sand.
That is what the desert widows did.
They made paper flowers

para llenar a los zapatos vacíos.
Una me entregó una mano de
un niño muerto
y al tomarla se convirtió
en una flor del viento.

to fill the empty shoes.
One of them gave me the hand of
a dead child,
and as I took it, it changed
into a flower of the wind.

C.K.C.

THE DEAD AND THE LIVING

MI NACIÓN Y LOS SISTEMAS DE CORREO

Dirección insuficiente,
casa deshabitada
voló como paloma en soledad
Ausente
Fallecido
Mutilado
Rehusado
Desconocido en los círculos sin salida
No existe tal nombre
DESAPARECIDO.

PRÓLOGO

Las desaparecidas se deslizaron entre los sueños. Me vigilaban, a
veces me despertaban acariciándome, más que nada me pedían que no
las olvidara. Así fueron creciendo estas Zonas del dolor. Ellas, las
mujeres enterradas pero siempre vivas fabricaron las urdimbres de mis
palabras que en la humildad de la impotencia buscaron claridades y
voces.

Las zonas del dolor representan la travesía de las enterradas, como
también la travesía de las madres buscadoras. Las zonas del dolor son
nuestras, son oscuras, y a veces demasiado olvidadizas. Por eso yo
las escribí, porque quise acompañar a mis hermanas muertas.

MY COUNTRY AND THE POSTAL SYSTEM

Address Insufficient,
house uninhabited
flew away like a lonely dove
Absent
Deceased
Mutilated
Refused
Unknown in circles without exit
Such a name doesn't exist
DISAPPEARED.

PROLOGUE

The disappeared women slipped in among dreams. They would watch
me, at times they would wake me up caressing me, more than anything
else they would ask me not to forget them. That's how these Zones of
Pain kept growing. The women, buried but still alive, wove the fabric of
my words that in the humility of helplessness sought for clear places
and voices.

The zones of pain represent the wandering of buried women and the
wandering of searching mothers. the zones of pain are ours, are dark,
and at times too easily slip the mind. For these reasons I wrote them
down, because I wish to accompany my dead sisters.

MEMORIAL DE LAS LOCAS EN LA PLAZA DE MAYO

— A la memoria de Marta Traba

No hay nada aquí,
la plaza, en silencios,
diminuta, azulada,
entre los cirios que se despliegan
como ajenos bultos
revolcándose,
encima de las piedras.

¿Hay alguien aquí?
Comienzan las peregrinaciones de las transparentes,
las procesiones,
las palabras de las ilusas,
son, dicen,
las locas de la Plaza de Mayo,
en busca de ojos,
de manos tibias,
en busca de un cuerpo,
de tus labios para jamás poseerte
para siempre llamarte
amado.

Agrietadas, enjutas,
orando,
gritando de rabia,
preguntando
encima de los bultos
más allá de los ecos,
las locas, en Buenos Aires, El Salvador,
en Treblinka
quieren saber
necesitan saber,
¿dónde están los hijos de los diecisiete?
¿los padres-esposos?

REMEMBERING THE MADWOMEN OF THE PLAZA DE MAYO

—In memory of Marta Traba

There is nothing here,
the plaza, silent,
small, blue,
in the center of candles that fan out
like alien shapes
circling
over the stones.

Is there anyone here?
It begins, the pilgrimage of the invisible ones
the procession,
the words of the deluded women,
they are, it is said,
the madwomen of the Plaza de Mayo,
searching for eyes,
for warm hands,
searching for a body,
for your lips, not to possess you
but so I can always call you
beloved.

Wrinkled, skeletal,
praying,
screaming in rage,
questioning
above the shapes
beyond the echoes,
the madwomen, in Buenos Aires, in El Salvador,
in Treblinka
want to know,
have to know,
where are their seventeen-year-old sons?
their husbands, fathers of their children?

¿los novios de las más niñas?
¿acaso son los arrojados al río maloliente de los justos?

Se acercan,
míralas como vuelan las brujas de la verdad
míralas como la lluvia arrastra sus lánguidos y demenciales cabellos,
mírales los pies, tan pequeños para arrastrar el dolor del abandono,
el dolor de la indiferencia.

Las locas,
amarrando la fotografía demolida, arrugada, borroneada,
vacía de la memoria incierta
la fotografía cautiva
¿por quién? ¿para quién?
mira el silencio en la plaza de las locas, mira como la tierra
se esconde,
se enmudece,
se revuelca como una muerta herida que sólo
quiere descansar,
y es sólo silencio quien acude a oírlas,
es el silencio
de la plaza quien oye
las fotografías
de los olvidados
presentes.

the boyfriends of the youngest girls?
were they perhaps thrown into the fetid river of their judges?

They come near,
look at them how they flutter, the witches of truth,
look at them how the rain plasters down their listless and demented hair
look at their feet, how small they are to bear the pain of abandonment,
the pain of indifference.

The madwomen
holding fast to a photograph, tattered, wrinkled, faded,
empty of uncertain memory
captive photograph
by whom? for whom?
look at the silence in the plaza of the madwomen, look how the earth
scurries to hide,
tires,
falls back like one mortally wounded who only
wishes for rest,
and so it is only silence that comes to hear them
it is the silence
of the plaza
that listens to the photographs
of the forgotten ones
here present.

C.F.

CORDILLERAS

Para Raúl Zurita

Ella le lavó la cara,
buscó la familiaridad
de sus ojos,
acarició el desprendido cabello de
humos y reacios matorrales,
limpió asustada las
heridas abiertas
como los nombres
boca abajo tras
los cauces
de un río.

Ella, regresó lejana
en la letanía
del Adiós
sola, solísima
a una casa perdida
entre las cordilleras
de
Chile.

MOUNTAINS

for *Raúl Zurita*

She washed his face
she sought the familiar look
in his eyes,
she stroked his hair, a loosened mass of
smoke and stubborn tanglewood,
she cleaned out, horrified, the
open wounds
like names left
face down
in a riverbed.

She went back, distant
in the litany
of leave-taking,
alone, all alone,
to a house lost
out among
the mountain lands
of
Chile.

RECORDAR

Recordar no era peligroso,
porque en el silencio
ella podía ser una
bóveda abierta,
una selva benigna para
inventar.
Y ella recordaba la luz atravesando su cuerpo desnudo frente a un trozo
azul de tiempo.
Recordaba las palabras que su boca, como el humo, iban trazando
en los paseos y murmullos por una ciudad sin mar.

Cuánto le gustaba recordar,
la monótona travesía por
la playa
o las sombras de arena que
seguían sus huellas.
Ella, recordaba el rumbo
incierto de las mareas
y entre las horas, pronunciaba
el movimiento de las olas,
los besos contra el roquerío
todo, para poder recordar: llamar-amar-escribir.

En sus inmensos cuadernos, entre sus dedos,
ella memorizaba aquellos nombres de
todos los días,
aquellos mansos transeúntes
que desaparecieron
pero no de su recuerdo,
porque ella, llamaba, gritaba y sus delgadas manos escribían
el mensaje de los papiros,
en las botellas azules
que navegaban no a una deriva.

REMEMBERING

Remembering wasn't dangerous,
because in silence
she could be an
open vault,
a jungle harmless
to invent.
And she remembered light slicing through his naked body against
a blue swatch of time.
She remembered the words his mouth, like smoke, traced out,
down the walkways and murmurs, across the city with no sea.

How she liked remembering
the monotonous stroll along
the beach
or the sandy shadows
following her tracks.
She recalled the shifting
pathways of the tides
and, in those hours, pronounced
the movement of the waves
kisses up against the rocks
everything, just to keep remembering: calling-loving-writing.

In her great long journals, in between her fingers,
she memorized those ordinary
names,
those mild-mannered passers-by
who disappeared
but not from her memory,
because she called out, screamed, and her thin hands wrote
the message of papyrus scrolls
into the blue bottles
that sailed off, not just drifting on the sea.

Ella recordaba sus
viajes
por la piel antigua
del que la abandonó por la manía del olvido,
y ella, lo pensaba,
mandándole hebras doradas que se desprendían de la redondez
de un sueño,
soñado tantas veces
sólo para nombrarlo
soñándolo
sólo para
soñarlo
nombrándolo.

She remembered her
travels
across the ancient skin
of the one who abandoned her driven by oblivion
and she thought him back,
sending him gold filaments that peeled off from the roundness
of a dream
dreamed so often
just to name him
by dreaming him
just to dream him
by naming him.

N.L.

Cuando encendida la luz de la noche,
y el tiempo es una manta de agua viva,
y el cielo otro silencio aún más silencioso,
cuando las paredes retratan las trizaduras de la mala hora
y todas se duermen en las criptas del insomnio
entonces saco mi fotografía
hago el amor con ella,
la desvisto,
la bailo,
la oigo,
acariciándola,
amándola muy así como en un aire muy dulce,
entonces,
le hablo,
le digo: qué bueno que has regresado de los infiernos,
hace tanto tiempo
que no nos vemos;
tanto tiempo sin verte
y la coloco junto
a mi pecho,
me pongo a bailar
con mi muerto
y me pongo a soñar con
mi foto.

When the evening light burns
and time is a blanket of living water,
and the sky another silence even more silent,
when the walls depict the shredded fragments of the evil hour
and everyone falls asleep in the crypts of insomnia
then I take out my photograph
I make love to it,
I undress it,
I dance with it,
I hear it,
caressing it,
and loving it much like a spring of fresh water,
then
I talk to it,
and say: how wonderful that you have returned from hell,
it has been a long time
since we have seen each other;
so much time without seeing you
and I place it close
to my chest,
and I begin to dance
with my dead one
and I begin to dream with
my photo.

Vacíos para siempre han quedado
los armarios, y ella conversa en la orilla de una cama
que se escurre, flota, y es un oficio de tinieblas,
donde el cuerpo ido deja una huella que corroe
y ella, arqueada, palpa las camisas
y palpa las fotografías
de los nobles días de la vida.
Entonces se pone
a cantar
a pesar de las densas neblinas,
entonces se pone a cantar.

The closets have remained empty forever,
and she converses at the edge of a bed
that glides, floats, and is a ritual of darkness
where the absent body leaves an impression that corrodes,
and she, crouching, caresses the shirts,
and caresses the photographs
of the noble days of life.
And then she begins
to sing,
in spite of the dense mist,
then she begins to sing.

C.K.C.

AUSCHWITZ

I.

Y ahí estábamos
agazapados
inclinados
sumergidos
en esa honda pena
en los aposentos
de aquellos
gases silenciosos
parecidos a la
lava de volcanes
cancerosos.

II.

Y no llorábamos
y no cantábamos
rezábamos con las
dudas milenarias
de un pueblo desnudo
y heroico en maldiciones,
y ahí estábamos
en los cuartos
de gas
en la soledad misma
de las noches petrificadas,
silenciosas
y alguien extendía sus brazos
en el racimo mismo oscuro del miedo.

AUSCHWITZ

I.

And there we were
crouched down
bent over
sunk
in that deep pain
in the chambers
of those soundless gases
like
lava from cancerous
volcanoes.

II.

And we were not crying,
we were not singing:
we were praying with the age-old doubts
of a people naked
and heroic in damnation,
and there we were
in the gas
chambers
in the loneliness
of petrified, silent
nights
and someone stretched out their arms
into the dark florescence of fear itself.

R.S.

UNA FIEL VECINA

I.

La mujer de Sarajevo
sueña con las costas,
las mariposas azules sobre las colinas.
Dicen que hay tanto olor a muerte,
que ayer había cuarenta muertos
entre los escombros
y ella ya no llora ni pregunta
tampoco tiene miedo,
pero le gustaría oler el mar.

II.

Si tan sólo pudiese
llegar al mar,
ver las alondras
¿habrá alondras a la orilla de la playa?
se pregunta.
La mujer de Sarajevo
sólo desea llegar al fin de las costas.
Quiere el latido de las olas.
No quiere el latido en el corazón
de los vivos
que están muertos
o los muertos que parecen vivos.

III.

La guerra ya no parece guerra.
No será la ilusión de los vivos.
A nadie le importa la mujer de Sarajevo,
ni sus palabras
ni la flor como campana
tras las ventanas
agujereadas.

A LOYAL NEIGHBOR

I.

The woman from Sarajevo
dreams of seacoasts,
the blue butterflies over the hills.
They say that it smells so much of death,
that yesterday there were forty dead
among the ruins
and now she no longer cries nor questions
and neither is she afraid,
but she would like to smell the sea.

II.

If only she could reach the sea,
see the larks:
Will there be larks at the edge of the beach?
she wonders.
The woman from Sarajevo
only wishes to reach the seacoasts.
She desires the beat of the waves.
She does not wish for the beat of the heart
of the living
who are dead
or the dead who seem to be living.

III.

The war no longer seems a war.
It will not be the illusion of the living.
Nobody cares about the woman from Sarajevo,
not her words
or the flower like a bell
behind the windows
riddled with holes.

IV.

La muerte es una fiel vecina.
Está en las hierbas putrefactas del jardín
está en el cielo agujereado,
pero no en el mar.

V.

La mujer de Sarajevo sueña con las costas.
Quiere que el mar la unte,
que le lave ese olor a sangre,
ese olor a sangre en la garganta.

IV.
Death is a loyal neighbor.
She is in the garden's rotting grass;
she is in the perforated sky
but not in the sea.

V.
The woman from Sarajevo dreams of seacoasts.
She wants the sea to anoint her,
to wash away that smell of blood,
that smell of blood in the throat.

M.G.B.

UNA AUSENCIA DE SOMBRAS

I.
Más allá de las sombras
donde mora el viento
entre los extraños,
en las lejanías del reino
nublado del miedo,
están ellos
los desaparecidos
entre las sombras
en los intersticios del sueño.

II.
Es posible oírlos entre
las ramas muertas,
entre ellos se acarician y reconocen,
han dejado las luces encendidas de la foresta
y las velas del amanecer y el amor.

III.
Más allá de la provincia
hay una ausencia,
una presencia de sombras
y de historias.

IV.
No les temas,
acércate a ellos
con la paz de la ternura,
sin rigor sin fuegos fatuos.
Más allá de la sombra
en las trizaduras
del viento,
moran ellos y nosotros
en el reino de la ausencia.

AN ABSENCE OF SHADOWS

I.
Beyond the shadows
where the wind dwells
among strangers,
in far away kingdoms
clouded in fear,
the disappeared
are among the shadows
in the intervals of dream.

II.
It's possible to hear them among
the dead branches,
they caress and recognize each other,
having left behind the burning
lights of the forest
and the tapers of dawn and love.

III.
Beyond the province
there is an absence,
a presence of shadows
and histories.

IV.
Don't fear them,
approach them
with gentle peacefulness,
without vehemence and senseless rage.
Beyond the shadows
in the streaming gusts
of wind,
they and we dwell
in the kingdom of absences.

RENEÉ EPPELBAUM

Como en un vacío circular
silencioso
sola ha quedado
la Plaza de Mayo sin ti,
viajera infinita
compañera de los muertos
y de los vivos.

Descansarás en paz
Reneé Eppelbaum
en las puertas de un cielo imaginario
¿vendrá algún ángel para aliviar tu vuelo?

Sola ha quedado
la Plaza de Mayo sin tus pasos lentos y cautelosos
sin tus ojos acostumbrados
a dialogar con la muerte.

Dicen que te has muerto, Reneé,
pero hoy he salido a buscarte entre los jacarandas,
entre la sombra de todas las ausencias.

Y tu voz me ha cantado
como un aire de la noche
y de pronto has estado entre las hojas muertas
y tu memoria se ha vuelto
en un don
lleno de claridades
y tus manos
anillo
alianzas
en esta plaza que es
tuya
que te nombra

RENEÉ EPPELBAUM

As in a circular
silent hollow space,
the Plaza de Mayo
has become lonely without you,
infinite traveler,
companion of the dead
and the living.

You will rest in peace,
Reneé Eppelbaum,
at the gates of an imaginary heaven.
Will some angel come to relieve your flight?

The Plaza de Mayo
has become lonely without your deliberate and cautious steps,
without your eyes accustomed
to speaking with death.

They say that you have died, Reneé,
but today I have gone out to look for you among the jacarandas,
among the shadows of all the absences.

And your voice has sung to me
like an evening breeze
and suddenly you have been among the dead leaves
and your memory has returned
with a touch of grace
filled with clarity
and your hands
ring
alliances
in this plaza that is
yours,
that names you,

estás aquí
Reneé visible
circular
danzarina.

Dicen que te has muerto, Reneé,
pero aquí he venido a buscarte
donde alguien rozó mi hombro
y encontró mis manos.

you are here, Reneé,
visible,
circular,
dancing.

They say that you have died, Reneé,
but I have come to look for you here
where someone rubbed my shoulder
and found my hands.

PISAGUA

Aquel mudo y hablado desierto
guardó sus cuerpos:
cabezas decapitadas,
manos arqueadas por una soga gris.
El desierto preservó sus vidas.
Por muchos años fue como la nieve eterna,
cuidadosa de lo que se oculta
bajo la tierra.
En la hipnótica aridez,
los muertos aún vivían
para contarte la historia.

FLORES NOCTURNAS

Cauta y sin ceremonias,
pone en evidencia sus recuerdos:
lutos antiguos,
ausencias de voces.
Riega las flores
nocturnas
del desierto
que se posan
en sus manos
para vigilar su tristeza.

PISAGUA

That mute yet mentioned desert
protected the
decapitated heads,
hands encircled by a gray rope.
The desert preserved their lives.
For many years it was like an eternal snow,
caring for what hides
beneath the earth.
In the hypnotic dryness,
the dead lingered
to tell you the story.

NOCTURNAL FLOWERS

Cautious and without ceremony,
she reveals her memories:
ancient sorrows,
absence of voices.
She waters
the nocturnal flowers
of the desert
that alight
on her hands,
to guard her sadness.

C.K.C.

THRESHOLDS
OF DREAM AND DESIRE

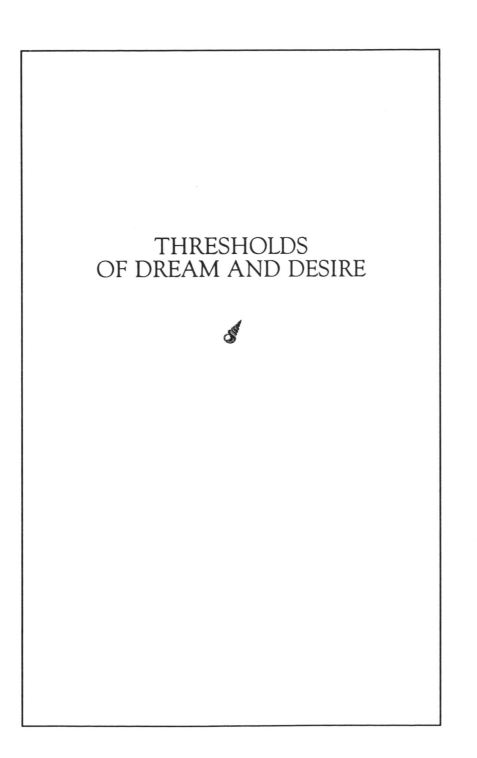

LEJOS

Mi país es un astillero
anclado dentro de mí
curvándose por entre
las rodillas y la piel
aún húmeda de sol.
Mi país es una frazada de estrellas como viruelas
una rapsodia de voces nulas
que aparecen para penar a la luna
por el pellejo raptado
a plena luz.

Mi país es un frasco azul
oculto y radiante como el mar
o la sombra de tus ojos
que nunca serán azules.

Mi país es un hombre
a quién amé
y cuando me besaba
mis piernas eran una lluvia
como un bosque o una
frontera de agua santa.

Mi país es color de humo
y planchas de carbón
que adormecidas empañan
las casas de adobe.

Mi país
es mi casa con las llaves
ocultas esperándome,
en la playa.

FAR AWAY

My country is a slender pier
anchored inside me
curving between
my knees and skin
still damp from the sun.
My country is a tatter of stars like pockmarks
a rhapsody of useless voices
that come out to mourn the moon
through the ravished pelt
of plain daylight.

My country is a blue vial
hidden and radiant as the sea
or the shadow of your eyes
that never will be blue.

My country is a man
whom I loved
and when he kissed me
my legs turned to rain
to a grove
to a boundary of holy water.

My country is the color of smoke
and coal-heated irons
that drowsily envelop
the houses of adobe.

My country
is my house with the keys
hidden waiting for me,
on the beach.

C.F.

CARIBE HILTON

La noche, alada céntrica
como una fantasía de palmeras
es ligera, acuosa
tropezando con la verde redondez marina
del agua,
del mar Caribe
que encendido y oscuro
posando, fotogénico
yace,
aguarda.
A lo lejos se ocultan los lagartos,
flores borrosas y largas colas de rata se descuelgan de las arenas.

Hambrientos
con un terco caminar entre las olas
acechan tras los cristales cóncavos aguardan
los elásticos movimientos
de melenas rubias
de dentaduras completas
de piernas teñidas por un sol ajeno:
sol de tierras mordidas.

Salsa cha cha salsa,
gafas ensordecedoras
salsa,
de sacerdotes blancos
consumiendo los oráculos dorados
de una memoria ajena
ellos bailan
con el hielo entre los labios
ligeramente hundidos como látigos.

A lo lejos,
en la otra costa

CARIBE HILTON

The night, a swirl of city
like a palm-frond fantasy
is loose and liquid
colliding with the wraparound
green sea:
the water
the Caribbean
lit up, darkened
best side to the camera
lying there in wait.
In the distance the alligators hide,
blurry flowers and long rats' tails hang from the sand.

Hungry
pushing their way through the waves
they lurk behind warped windowpanes, eying
the supple bounce
of big blond heads of hair
of flawless smiles
of legs dyed bronze on other people's sunshines
the sunshine of leached lands.

Salsa cha cha salsa
deafening eyeglasses
salsa,
white priests
eating up the golden oracles
of someone else's memory
they dance
with ice between their lips
slightly sunken in like whips.

A ways off
on the other coast

dos se hunden
ondulados queriéndose
mordiéndose lentamente
entre el traicionero rumor de palmeras y palmas
que no favorecen
el azar de los descalzos.

Ellos asediando las estrellas hundidas del Caribe Hilton y un espectro
de Miss Monroe,
ellos como ráfagas incendiadas comiéndose en las arenas del Caribe
arenas de latas deshechas
ellos clarividentes brillan

y el ron aún no
apaga esa sed
de esa
otra voz.

a couple plunges into
undulating loving
nibbling slowly
amid the slithery sounds of palms and palm fronds
never too kind to
the fortunes of the barefoot.

The couple stalks the sunken stars of the Caribe Hilton and a spectre
of Miss Monroe
like burning blasts of wind devouring one another on Caribbean sands
sands of washed-up cans
they gleam with glimpses of the future

and not even rum
can slake that thirst
of that
other voice.

INVIERNO EN LA PLAZA DE MAYO

Como en un prisma
me contemplo,
entre el equinoccio
de mi piel
y mis manos
que repetidas e incesantes
se abrazan,
o reparten
maíz a las palomas,
que no ocultan
los gestos:
alimentar palomas reposar las yemas
en tu cabello
desterrador de pesadillas.

Tú también sigues
el destino de mis
manos,
en este día
donde las aves
cantan
en la
Plaza
de Mayo.

WINTER IN THE PLAZA DE MAYO

As if in a prism
I study myself
from the equinox
of my skin
to my hands
over and over
clasping together
or throwing out
corn to the pigeons
who make no secret of their moves;
to feed the pigeons
to rest the fingertips
against your hair
that casts out nightmares.

You share
a common future with my
hands
on this day
when birds
are singing
in the
Plaza de Mayo.

N.L.

LAS FLORES AMARILLAS

Las flores amarillas
destapadas reposando sobre las yerbas sedosas
parecen ser las faldas que el viento levanta y trepa
y soplan en una luz ténue de gracias secretas
y adivinan los sueños de los desvalidos
espectadores
de las mujeres solísimas
que buscan una flor amarilla de la amanecida
en sus contornos
que buscan una ráfaga de amarillos
para las tumbas
sin nombre.

TOCANDO EL CIELO

Más importante que recordar
los nombres
es saber que la felicidad y el sosiego
están a la orilla,
los pies
casi tocando el agua
que es el cielo.

THE YELLOW FLOWERS

The yellow flowers
uncovered and resting on the silken grass
seem like skirts that the wind lifts and mounts
and they blow in a tenuous light of secret graces,
foretelling the dreams for the unprotected
spectators,
of the very lonely women
who watch from their outposts
for a yellow flower of dawn,
who look for a gust of yellow blossoms
for the tombs
of the nameless.

C.K.C.

TOUCHING THE SKY

More important than remembering
names
is to know that happiness and tranquility
lie at the shore,
the feet
almost touching water
which is sky.

C.F.

VALPARAÍSO

I.
En Valparaíso
el viento adelgazando las
miradas,
los duendes
enroscándose
por los cerros
y el embrujo
el aire
tan dulce
de una ciudad
desordenada
enterrada
entre los terremotos
y las alianzas marinas.

II.
Valparaíso,
yo te amo
y mientras te hablo
eres una hebra azul,
un sonido
que ilumina
a los faros,
al recato
de los prófugos
a los que se enlazan
a media luz entre
los barcos abandonados
soñándose con los
amores de una noche fantasma enloquecida divagadora.

VALPARAÍSO

I.

In Valparaíso
the wind blowing off
glances,
wind-spirits
weaving their way
through the hills,
and the gentle
sweet-smelling air
is the spell
of a city
disordered
buried
amid earthquakes
and their oceanic allies.

II.

Valparaíso
I love you
and even as I speak of you
you are a blue
thread,
a sound illuminating
lighthouses,
a safe harbor
for fugitives,
those who embrace each other
in the half-light amongst
abandoned ships
dreaming of
loves on a wild spectral wandering night.

ISLA NEGRA

En Isla Negra
Pablo Neruda
camina por el agua:
de sus pies brotan
anémonas violetas,
victoriosas
mariposas,
soñolientas
y redondas.
En Isla Negra
Don Pablo
camina
danzante, danzando,
sus pies son
dos campanas, vertiginosas y dulces;
su voz
una palabra
un manantial
un trozo de agua
descendiendo, hasta el origen
del cielo
que palpita.

ISLA NEGRA

On Isla Negra
Pablo Neruda
goes walking by the water:
violet sea anemones,
triumphant
butterflies,
asleep
and rounded,
gather at his feet.
On Isla Negra
Don Pablo
strolls about,
a dancer, dancing,
his feet are
two giddy, sweet-sounding bells;
his voice
a word,
a clear spring,
a drop of water
falling from the throbbing
sky
to the origin of things.

                                        R.S.

SERPENTINAS

Si vinieras conmigo al Sur de Francia
veríamos las serpentinas de la luz,
el amanecer entre las lavandas
y los trigales imaginarios.

Si vinieras conmigo al Sur de Francia
te desnudarías por las tardes,
cuando las luz es un recado,
una voz transfigurada
por los azules y malvas.
Te regalaría grullas, garzas salvajes,
las hierbas del Sur de Francia
traídas de una tierra festejada y ebria.
Haría un banquete.
Entre tus manos
como palomas como espejos
donde nada se pierde en la mirada
victoriosa del deseo.

Y si estuviéramos en el Sur de Francia
iríamos a la casa de piedra
donde no hay llaves en los cuartos,
tan sólo ventanas y musgos,
veranos incandescentes.
Pasaríamos la noche entre los pastos.
Soñaríamos con el cielo que parece un bosque de hadas,
tu piel también sería un follaje que quema
y ama,
tus manos encendidas como el girasol perpetuo
que no quiere la noche y su
vaticinio de sombras.

Si estuviéramos en el Sur de Francia
haría de tu cuerpo un campo de lavandas.

STREAMERS OF LIGHT

If you came with me to the South of France
we would see streamers of light
at daybreak amidst the lavender
and imaginary wheat fields.

If you came with me to the South of France
you would undress in the afternoons
when the light is a message,
a voice transfigured
by blues and mauves.
I would give you cranes, wild herons,
herbs of the South of France
brought from a joyous and drunken earth.
I would prepare a banquet.
In your hands,
like doves, like mirrors
where nothing is lost in the victorious
gaze of desire.

And if we were in the South of France
we would go to the stone house,
where the rooms have no keys
but only windows and moss
incandescent summers.
We would spend the night among the grasses.
We would dream of the sky that seems
an enchanted forest
your skin, too, would be foliage that burns
and loves
your blazing hands like the eternal sunflower
that shuns the night and its prophecy of shadows.

If we were in the South of France
I would make your body into a field of lavender.

TRIGALES

I.

He regresado a los trigales
para contemplar la suave mudez sobre los
campos,
para contemplar el tiempo de las fragancias.
Mi caballete es un lienzo espigado,
distante y amarillo,
carcomido por el desamor.
Contemplo el césped
que fue la morada de
mis antepasados,
de los vagabundos
aquí en St. Paul.

II.

He regresado a los trigales cegados,
con mis manos llenas de jacintos y jazmines
e hibiscos envenenados.
Descanso,
me retiro del enjambre de amarillos.
Soy un cuerpo entre las sombras,
a mi alrededor se congregan los pájaros.

WHEATFIELDS

I.

I have come back to the wheatfields
to contemplate the soft muteness of the
fields,
to contemplate the time of fragrances
my easel is a sprouting canvas,
distant and yellow,
ravaged by rejection
I contemplate the grass
that was the home of
all of my ancestors,
of the vagrants
here in St. Paul's.

II.

I have come back to the blinded wheatfields
with my hands full of hyacinths and jasmine
and poisoned hibiscus.
I rest
I withdraw from the swarm of yellows
I am a body among the shadows
birds gather around me.

M.B.

AMAPOLAS

I.
Amapolas rojizas,
almidonadas,
como ángeles carmesíes
recostados sobre los campos,
haciendo todos los vuelos posibles.
Amapolas como las trizaduras
del cuerpo de las
mujeres amándose en soledades.

II.
Amapolas florecidas
entre las ausencias de los caminos.
Amapolas rosas, rosadas, conmovidas y desprevenidas
ante los capullos
florecidos.
Amapolas a la hora de las tibiezas,
hebras rojizas al paso de las golondrinas,
señalando lo más silvestre del campo.
Amapolas, como mujeres del campo
rojizas, enamoradas, abiertas
como las cúpulas más hondas del placer.

POPPIES

I.
Flaming poppies,
starched,
like crimson angels
resting over the fields,
making all flights possible.
Poppies like the shreddings
of the bodies of
women loving themselves in solitude.

II.
Blooming poppies
in the absence of roads.
Poppies red, pink, so moving so awe inspiring
before those flowering
cocoons.
Poppies at the hour of warmth
carmine fibers with the passing of swallows,
signaling the wilderness of the fields.
Poppies, like women of the field
damask, in love, open
like the deepest cupolas of pleasure.

M.B.G.

FLORES NOCTURNAS

Nocturnas, ceremoniosas
crecen, son, gimen como lenguas silenciosas
para florecer como un pubis rosado,
consagradas al destino de las estaciones.
Las flores nocturnas del desierto
se encienden como una ceremonia
más allá de los asombros.

NOCTURNAL FLOWERS

Nocturnal, ceremonial
they grow, exist, whimper like silent tongues
in order to flower like a pink pubis,
consecrated to the fate of the seasons.
Nocturnal flowers of the desert
light up like a ceremony
beyond astonishment.

EL TIEMPO CLARO DEL AMOR

I.

Como en el tiempo
claro del amor,
regresé al desierto.
La noche era un blanco rebozo
de hebras azules,
titilantes;
mi voz era la voz
del horizonte.
Todo era claro, clarividente.
Nada oscuro había
en el fondo de las cosas.

II.

Regresé sola y descalza,
vestida entre las arenas.
Tanta luz había en mis espaldas.
Negué la oscuridad cóncava de las ciudades,
la avaricia.

III.

El silencio era
la gran ternura
que nunca tuve
y el viento,
las palabras de Dios.

LOVE'S CLEAR TIME

I.

In love's clear
time,
I returned to the desert.
the night was a white shawl
of shimmering
blue threads;
my voice was the voice
of the horizon.
Everything was clear, clairvoyant.
nothing was obscure
in the depth of things.

II.

I returned barefoot and alone,
dressed up among the sands.
There was so much light on my back.
I denied the concave darkness of cities,
the greed.

III.

Silence was
the great tenderness
I never had,
and the wind,
the words of God.

C.K.C.

ALCHEMIES OF THE HEART

HOGUERAS

Mi cabeza,
es una medusa.
Una hoguera
de girasoles
mientras me
lavas los
cabellos.

DESEO

Deseo,
cosquilla
leve,
vacilante.
Costra dorada
durmiente
indomable
acurrucándose
por la
piel.

BONFIRES

My head
is a jellyfish.
A giant mass
of sunflowers set afire
when you
wash my
hair.

DESIRE

Desire,
a gentle,
hesitant
tickle,
a golden crust
asleep
untamable
snuggling
nestled
in the skin.

SONIDOS-SUEÑOS

Los sonidos del otoño,
son sahumerios amarillos
retrocediendo en
las navajas de
la infancia,
donde los ruidos ajenos
llenos de mariposas y hojas
eran las orgías peligrosas
de niños desabrigados.

Los sonidos del
otoño, son las
calles de mi ciudad,
o el olor de tu nuca inclinada
rodando triunfante
sobre un abanico de
hojas parecidas
a todos los cabellos,
a todos los sonidos,
tibios, amarantas, espesos
de los lechos
en el
otoño.

DREAM SOUNDS

The sounds of autumn
are yellow censers
folding back into
the knives of
childhood,
where outsider sounds
full of butterflies and leaves
were the dangerous orgies
of children unprotected from the cold.

The sounds of autumn are the
streets of my city,
or the smell at the scruff of your neck
rolling in triumph
across a fan of
leaves just like
all hair,
all sounds,
warm,
just barely warm, deep purple, dense,
of beds
in autumn.

N.L.

AZÚCAR

Antigua y distante
te fueron urdiendo
de tus hojas pardas, teñidas por la luz
de las tinieblas,
de las espesuras,
clara, te volvieron
como planta clarividente
presagiando el destino
de los que te cortaron
para endulzar el paladar
apestado de los robadores de vidas y de almas
de los que con navajas
vigilaban
para que te sacaran el alma,
la sustancia intrépida
de tus hojas.

Ya los mercaderes
invasores,
tentados por el oro delirante
de tu caña
hicieron de tí,
una patria, Hispaniola,
jaspeada Cuba,
hierba de las
angustias,
el destino de los negros descalzos,
los desatados en la pena de las sombras,
pero tú
azúcar,
les enseñaste de canciones y caricias
ardías cuando te humedecían sus lenguas
atareadas en tu regazo
porque eras fecunda

SUGAR CANE

In ancient remote times
they were contriving you.
From your dark leaves, tinted by the light
of darkness
and from the denseness,
they made you clear
like a clairvoyant plant
foreseeing the fate
of those who cut you
to sweeten the spoiled
palates of the robbers of lives and souls
of those with knives who
kept watch
to make sure your soul was extracted,
the dauntless substance
of your leaves.

Already the invading
merchants
tempted by the delirious gold
of your canes
made of you
a country, Hispaniola
multi-colored Cuba,
plant of
anguish,
the destiny of barefoot
blacks, wild in the grieving shadows,
but you,
sugar cane,
taught them songs and caresses,
blazed when their tongues moistened you
busy up in your lap
bountiful amid the tears

dulcísima entre las lágrimas
y sabías como las generosas mujeres
regresar a la abismante delicia del paladar
azúcar clara, clarísima
mulata parda
danzarina
encantada
ofrenda misteriosa para los ajenos señores
los hidalgos en enormes palabras y extranjerías huérfanas,
pero tú
nunca te dejaste tentar en lo más adentro de tus navajas
y fuiste la hierba
que endulzaba la tristeza,
que cantaba en los sorbos de la risa,
entre los dedales de la noche
blanquísima, oscurecida, anochecida, parda
azúcar.

and you always knew like big-hearted women
to return to the amazing delight of taste
white sugar, snow white,
dark mulatto girl
dancing girl
bewitched
mysterious offering for foreign gentlemen
the hidalgos of outsized words and alien expressions
but you
never let knives touch your inmost essence
you were the plant
that sweetened sadness,
sang between sips of laughter
amid the labyrinths of night
most white, shaded, nightdark, warm brown
sugar.

YERBA MATE

I.

Yerba mate,
sagrada, hospitalaria, amiga
de los hambrientos,
de los nobles viajeros en oscuras
latitudes
como las forestas y el carbón
eres,
compañera de siempre,
la bebida de velorios,
y regresos a la vida
curándonos en los sorbos
pausados
de las tristezas
y de las quebraduras del tiempo,
los dolores del alma.

II.

Yerba mate,
secada, soleada siempre viva,
despertadora de gallos,
fiel guardiana de fértiles maderas,
sombra de los asombros,
lucidez de los limoneros,
ahí estás como una joya de musgos
silbando jadeante al compás del tiempo
y el agua hervida.

III.

Yerba mate:
muy pocos entibian tus secretos
los misterios de la bombilla,
una hoja de mate
balanceándose

YERBA MATE

I.

Yerba mate,
sacred, hospitable, friend
to the hungry,
to noble travelers in dark
latitudes
like forests and coal
you are
a constant companion,
the beverage of wakes
and returns to life
curing us with unhurried
sips
of the sadness
and ruptures of time,
the anguish of the soul.

II.

Yerba mate,
dry, sunny, always lively,
alarm clock for roosters,
true guardian of fertile woodlands,
shade of the amazed,
light of lemon groves,
you seem like a mossy jewel
whistling puffing to the rhythm of time
and boiling water.

III.

Yerba mate:
few master your secrets
the mysteries of the bombilla,
a leaf of mate
waving

sobre las palabras
haciendo historias,
soplando la vida en tus aromas.

IV.

Es el viento,
la abismante
silenciosa noche,
la nocturna infusión de tu color,
los hombres,
las mujeres,
acercándote a tí
en el paladar
conocido
de tu nombre:
yerba mate
hojas de noche,
de sueño y almíbar humilde
hojas de silencio
parecidas
al secreto
de la
pena.

above words
making stories
breathing life into your aromas.

IV.

It is the wind,
the self-absorbed
silent night,
the nocturnal infusion of your warmth,
men,
women,
coming close to you
through the taste
called by your name:
Yerba mate
leaves of night,
of dream and modest honey
leaves of silence resembling
the secret
of
sadness.

CHILE

Chiles rojísimos,
chile de fuego y suaves
coloridos mensajeros
de la vida que arde
y se hace fruta, ternura, dolor,
así eres tú
generosa silvestre, maga, planta,
ancha como el Chile mismo
verde como la espesura del amor
menuda como el comienzo de los niños
en Atziticán
en Xochilmilco
en Hyaxpetec
Michoacán, Anahuac
te alzas
para nutrir a los enfermos y llenarlos de mejorías
y ayudas a las parturientas,
porque tienes corazón de bruja benevolente
y cubres a los difuntos
con las hogueras de tus aromas
para que después de la vida
más allá de la muerte,
no sean tan solos y escasos
y así junto al cuerpo de los finados
el chili se pasa por la luz intrépida del aire,
y las fogatas se pueblan de chiles encendidos
y los muertos se mecen bailando como si
fueran ánimas felices
en purgatorios enrojecidos
porque también los nahuales
celebran estas historias
de muertos,
quien no puede dejar de comer chile verde,
chile jalapeño

CHILE PEPPER

Chiles redder than red
fiery chiles and smooth
colored messengers
of a life that burns
and turns into fruit, tenderness, pain,
that's what you are like
generous wild magical plant
as ancha, wide, as the other Chile
as green as deepest love
as small as the onset of children
in Atziticán
in Xochilmilco
in Hyaxpetec
Michoacán, Anahuac
you spring up
to nourish the sick and make them well again
and you aid women in childbirth,
because you have the heart of a benevolent witch
you also cover the dead
with bonfires of your aromas
so that after life
beyond death
they will not be so alone and in want
and that way beside the body of the defunct
chiles pass through the intrepid light of the air
the faggots are embued with flaming chiles
and the dead sway and dance as if
they were happy spirits
without red glowing purgatories
because the Nahuas also
celebrate these stories
of the dead
who cannot stop eating green chiles
jalapeños

chile pasado`
chile milchilli
chile pichichi
chile pimentos
chile paloma

Capiscum milenario
aún vives en la lengua
de tu gente,
aún te acercas entre las plantas, las flores
territoriales
porque no pudieron
extraer tu sabor de historia
y con la humildad de los sabios,
acompañas a la comida de
los pobres y los ricos,
de los mercaderes y los reyes
que obligaban a pagar tributos por tu presencia
capiscum milagroso
aún te desean fresco
porque tu alma no se puede almacenar ni secar
porque no te pueden convertir en paprika,
chile de chocolte,
chile de ramo
chile chipaya
chile gachupín
te bendigo
nos ayudas a respirar
a querer
a recordar
y de tu salsa
se ensalsa
la vida,
del paladar,
la lengua de mis pueblos.

pasados
milchillis
pinchis
pimentos
paloma chiles.

Capsicum milenario,
you still live in the tongue
of your people
you still appear among plants and flowers
of the region
because they could not
remove your savor of history,
and with the modesty of the wise
you accompany the meals
of rich and poor,
merchants and kings,
who obliged to pay tribute by your presence
miraculous capsicum
still prefer you fresh
because your soul cannot be stored, dried
or ground into paprika
chocolte chile
ramo chilpaya
gachupín
I bless you
you help us to breathe
to love
to remember
and your spiciness
adds spice to life
to the palate
and tongue of my people.

PECES

Saludo a los peces del mar
respetando su milenaria
genealogía,
sus danzas fugaces y suaves,
los colores que delatan
otros colores,
sus colas iridiscentes
parecidas a los cristales
de las adivinanzas.

Brindo un vaso
de agua
por todos los peces
todavía libres
por su elegante sangre fría
y sus simetrías perfectas.

FISH

I greet the fish of the sea
respecting their ancient lineage,
their swift, smooth dances,
their colors that reveal
other colors,
their tails iridescent
like the crystal balls
of fortune tellers.

I lift a glass
of water
to all the fish
still free,
to their elegant, cold blood,
their perfect symmetry.

C.F.

PRIMAVERA

Después de la noche que
se fuga,
brota, estalla
en pequeños fulgores,
el día,
la niebla haciendo coronas de fuego
y luz,
tus pies desnudos invitan a la danza a lo que la
tierra desviste y te deja
palpar, ser.
Brota desde ella
y desde tus comienzos
indicios, presagios
el gusto que asegura una permanencia
preciosa que sobrevive a la piedra
a las voces hondas que nos marean de silencio.

Llega deleitosa
clara vestida del amarillo
de los niños,
la primavera, como una memoria
del jazmín.
Tu cuerpo ya no te pertenece
es del aire
de los espejos del día
y tú aprendes a habitarte
en las fragancias
que antes la lluvia borraba.

Ahora todo
permanece,
la alegría es el público del alma
los ancianos visten los parques de voces nuevas,
los ángeles y los hombres juegan a las escondidas.

SPRING

After the fleeting
night,
daylight emerges,
explodes
in a small brilliance,
fog makes fiery
crowns,
your naked feet invite to dance prompting
the earth to undress allowing you
to touch, to exist.
From it
and from your beginnings arise
signs, omens,
the gesture assuring a precious
permanence outliving the stones,
the deep voices that make us dizzy with silence.

It arrives full of charms
radiantly dressed in children's
yellow,
spring, like a memory
of jasmine.
Your body is no longer yours,
it belongs to the air,
the mirrors of daylight,
and you learn to inhabit yourself
in fragrances
that rain previously erased.

Now everything
is present,
joy is the audience of the soul,
the elderly dress the parks with new voices,
angels and men hide and seek.

De pronto,
te gusta este planeta,
deseas esa convivencia entre
verdor y estrellas.

Reconoces el brote de los jacintos
que han regresado a tu casa
como regresan las palabras a tus manos.

Florece tu escritura entre los crisántemos
cada noche meditas y escribes
sobre las flores pequeñas,
palpas el hondo corazón de la noche y del día.

Breve es esta estación de música
aprendes a nombrar pájaros y flores,
el césped se llena de pequeñas hebras
y tu gloria las dibuja sobre tus palmas.

No es necesario pensar en el amor
éste se juega, se esconde
todo da paso al asombro
la oscuridad se fuga
de paso al sol,
al ritmo de las flores nocturnas y diurnas
se suma con el ahora, con el breve ardor del florecimiento
el ritmo perpetuo de esta estación
que llega como una mujer enamorada
ante todo su fragancia
antigua que se hace niña
como el origen de las madreselvas
como el comienzo de las fucsias sobre tus manos.

Suddenly
you like this planet,
you desire this coexistence among
the greenery and the stars.

You recognize the budding hyacinths
newly arrived at your home
like words returning to your hands.

Your writing blooms among the chrysanthemums,
each night you meditate and write
about the small flowers,
you feel the deep heart of night and day.

Brief is this season of music,
you learn to name birds and flowers,
the grass is filled with tender leaves
and your glory draws them on your palm.

No need to think about love
it is playful, it hides,
everything gives way to astonishment,
darkness fades
surrendering to the sun,
to the rhythm of flowers, nocturnal and diurnal
converging in the present, with brief flowering ardor
the perpetual rhythm of this season
arriving like a woman in love,
first her fragrance
so old she becomes a child,
like the origin of honeysuckle,
the beginnings of fuchsias over your hands.

VERANO

Irresistible en la lentitud más espesa
en el sopor que es la textura hundida
en las fragancias
el verano abrupto y lento
danzante como el leopardo
con la melódica extravaganza de las
mariposas,
se acomoda y permanece,
se instala soberano
en los días que son gestos,
sobre el césped húmedo,
la piel agradecida
por el desnudo.

Las mujeres acostumbradas
al cuerpo entre las penumbras,
se desnudan sin premura,
no hay cautela ante el sol
tan sólo palpar la piel,
imaginarse aún joven
con los cabellos haciendo del viento
una danza perpetua.

Las mujeres ancianas no se reconocen
en las terrazas, en los balcones
en las islas vestidas de blanco,
se asoman
la mirada se eleva,
son las de antes como un ahora dormido,
se imaginan sus pechos jóvenes,
agradecidas por la vida
que no envejece, que las desnuda
como a las novias
y es tal la alegría

SUMMER

Irresistible in its most deliberate slowness,
in a drowsiness of sunken textures,
in fragrances,
summer, abrupt and slow,
dancing like a leopard,
with the melodic extravagance of
butterflies,
settles and remains,
reigns supreme
in days of caresses
on damp grass,
the skin grateful
in its nakedness.

Accustomed to shadows,
women bare themselves
carelessly and without haste
before the sun,
feeling only their skin,
imagining being young,
their hair in
a perpetual dance with the wind.

Older women do not recognize themselves
in terraces, in balconies
in islands dressed in white,
they come out,
their gazes rise,
they are beings from another time like a sleeping present,
they imagine their breasts young,
grateful for a life
which does not grow old,
revealing them like brides.
And such is the joy

del despojo
de saberse aladas
ligeras de equipaje
aguardando la noche
del verano como ángeles satisfechos,
sentir que el aire como ellas también se desvanece,
que el tiempo es el recuerdo de otro tiempo.

Alrededor de ellas la luz,
generosa, pálida, desterrada.
La luz como un secreto en el interior de todas las
habitaciones donde la luz es la imagen que tan sólo
habita en la desmemoriada memoria.

El verano, el musgo creciendo sobre la longitud del cielo
dorado, un deleite para nuestros ojos,
horizontes como las palmas de nuestras manos.
Tu cuerpo fugaz sobre la hierba
extendido como el viento del azar
todo y nada acontece,
alrededor buhos y pájaros en una corona de fuego.

Desnuda, te pareces a todos,
y sueñas en los días que el
verano regresa
como la estación certera
como el amor después de las trizaduras
desquiciando en su luz
la textura viviente de la memoria.

Te miras ahora
sola y plena
tan sólo reconoces la
memoria de lo que ha sido
traviesa con el universo, audaz,
inoportuna en el orden,

of letting go,
having wings,
traveling light
waiting for summer's night,
like contented angels
feeling the air fading, just like them,
time is a memory of another time.

All around them, light,
generous, pale, in exile.
Light like a secret hidden in all
rooms where light is the image residing only in
the absent-minded memory.

Summer, moss growing over the golden span of the horizon,
a delight to our eyes,
horizons like the palms of our hands.
Your fleeting body over the grass
extended like the wind of chance,
everything and nothing happens,
around us owls and birds in a crown of fire.

Naked, you resemble everyone,
and dream of days
when summer returns
like a certain season,
like love after being shattered
forcing out in its light
the living texture of memory.

Now, you look at yourself,
alone and fulfilled,
recognizing only the
memory of what has been,
mischievous with the universe, audacious,
inopportune with orderliness,

aventurera en las ilusiones.

Extensa, extendida
el mar te rodea
el mar te cobija
cubre tus pechos,
tus piernas que palpitan
y devuelven la antigua forma de tu cuerpo.

Estás habitada por un día de verano
tan sólo un día
eterno en su justicia
donde las horas pierden su compostura.
eres luz,
cúpula de aire,
ráfaga clara
quieta como el arco iris,
te recorres
te amas
en el instante de hoy porque no hay otro.
Desnuda bailas
sonríes,
la arena deshace tus huellas
y tu nombre.

adventurer with hope.

Wide, expansive
the sea surrounds you,
the sea protects you,
covers your breasts,
your pulsating legs that
return the ancient form to your body.

You are inhabited by a summer's day.
just one day
in its eternal justice
where hours lose their composure.
You are light,
cupola of air,
clear gust
quiet like a rainbow,
you touch,
you love
in the instant that is today because there is no other.
Naked you dance,
smile,
sand erases your steps
and your name.

OTOÑO

Deslumbrada
avanzas hacia
la intemperie
se empequeñecen los días
atrás el verano plácido y lento.

Caminas y te alumbras
las encantaciones del amarillo
el destino ocre de los árboles
que generosos
construyen mantas claras
para bendecir tus pasos,
pasos sigilosos
una fuga entre las hojas.

Y es hondo el asombro
ante el paisaje que se inclina
sobre tus pies
sobre el otoño que corona
tus cabellos rojizos.

Danzas y caminas
rememoras
efímera es
la memoria
como el paso de una estación a otra,
simple y pasajera,
una palabra resbalándose
sobre la otra,
y amas este ritmo intermedio
esta luminosidad oscura
preámbulo de un invierno cauto
como las palabras
de los ancianos gratos y temorosos.

AUTUMN

Stunned,
you advance towards
the open air,
days grow short
leaving behind the slow and fluid summer.

You walk and illuminate
the incantations of yellow,
the ochre destiny of trees
that generously
weave clear tapestries,
blessing your steps,
silent steps,
fugitive among the leaves.

A deep wonderment
before the landscape that overhangs
your feet,
autumn crowns
your auburn hair.

You dance and walk
recalling
that memory is
ephemeral,
like the passage of one season to the next,
simple and drifting
one word sliding
over the other,
and you love that intermediate rhythm,
that dark luminosity
preamble to a cautious winter,
like words
of pleasant and fearful elders.

Te preguntas cómo serán las otras soledades
o cómo inclinarás la frente a la
llegada del invierno,
o interpretarás los sonidos del adíos.

En este otoño cuando
los parques son los dominios del fuego
que habitas en el bosque de las preguntas
en esta estación inquieta
que siempre rueda hacia abajo
que acaricia tus tobillos
como lo hacía el agua de todos los veranos.

Quieta te alejas
y te acercas
confundes el atardecer,
piensas en las castañas
en las historias de las hojas muertas,
eres la viajera entre el ocre
y anaranjado de tu mirada,
tibias tus manos
agradeces.

You wonder about those other silences,
or how you will lower your forehead
at the arrival of winter,
or interpret
the sounds of good-byes.

In autumn, when
parks are dominions of fire,
you inhabit a forest of questions,
in the restless season
always rolling downward
touching your ankles
like the water of every summer.

Quietly you walk away
and come closer,
you do not recognize the dusk,
you think of chestnuts
in the stories of dead leaves,
you are a traveler among the ochre
and orange of your gaze,
your hands warm,
you give thanks.

L .N.

INVIERNO

Lentas las horas, horas de estanque y detenidas
cadenciosas sin ira
ni fuga
las horas breves,
iluminadas por la lumbre que es
una historia quieta
lentas las horas del invierno,
estación de rescoldos
tiempo sosegado
luz breve que cae plena en la
oscuridad de todos los días
cada vez diminutos
y breves.

En la oscuridad
imaginamos la luz.
Llega así el huésped más habitual,
presagia huellas
indaga sobre los muertos,
indaga sobre las huellas de la sombra
y nos habita.

En estos días que parecen noches cóncavas,
tantas veces vacías y llenas de un vacío
el invierno y yo acechándonos
paliando el espacio del silencio y el bullicio del alma.

El frío es una grieta sobre los pechos,
yo busco la caricia, el nombre
tu cuerpo se acerca, es como un valle de luces efímeras
me acerco a él para recuperar la
sed, la luz, los presagios de la felicidad.

El invierno nos inunda de leves tristezas,

WINTER

Slow hours, stagnant and arrested hours,
rhythmic, without fury
or escape,
brief hours
illuminated by fire,
recounting a quiet story,
slow winter hours,
season of embers,
peaceful time,
brief light that falls fully
in the darkness of every day,
each time more tentative
and brief.

In darkness
we imagine light,
thus the usual guest arrives,
announcing footsteps,
inquiring about the dead,
about the vestiges of shadows
inhabiting us.

In these days resembling concave nights,
so many times emptied and filled with emptiness,
winter and I watching each other,
softening the space of silence and the ruckus of the soul.

Cold is a crevice over anchored breasts,
I search for a caress, a name
your body comes closer, it is like a valley of ephemeral lights.
I approach it to recover
thirst, light, omens of happiness.

Winter floods us with the presence of tender sadness,

abanicos diáfanos en penumbra
pero es esta la estación que suplica
el tiempo llano de paz.

El frío nos recorre
y tú te acercas para cubrirme,
eres el viento dulce que se posa en mis labios,
y a veces me hace recordar los escombros sobre las tumbas
o las novias heladas atravesando las planicies
en la perpetua fuga de la muerte.

Es esta la estación de la memoria
y yo, encendida entre las velas melodiosas,
rezo, canto, me desdoblo y celebro
en este tiempo las noches largas
de las lunas imprecisas.

Es en la hora del invierno el tiempo del sur,
fragmento de geografía inconclusa
donde los rostros se aparecen sobre la nieve
más allá del viento, más allá del crepitar del fuego.
Son los rostros que exigen la longevidad del recuerdo,
crepitan como una flor sobre el fuego
y es en este fuego que jamás es fatuo,
que yo también te amo.

Tu cuerpo junto al mío
una llama perpetua,
una huella sobre los dominios de las sombras
y la memoria que rescata y canta.

Es en este invierno
donde llega la resurección de las hojas,
el tiempo que acontece
la mirada sobre los espejos de hielo,
estación malévola y bella,

diaphanous fans in semidarkness,
but this is the imploring season,
the unassuming time of peace.

Cold envelops us
and you come to cover me.
You are a sweet wind lighting on my lips,
sometimes reminding me of rubble over the tombs
or frozen brides crossing the plains
in a perpetual escape from death.

This is the season of memory
and I, illuminated among the melodious candles,
pray, sing, unfold and celebrate
in this season of long nights,
uncertain moons.

It is in the hour of winter, the Southern time,
fragment of unfinished geography,
where faces appear on the snow
beyond the wind, beyond the crackling fire.
They are faces that demand the longevity of remembrance,
they crackle like a flower over fire
and in this fire, ever conceited,
I love you.

Your body next to mine
a perpetual flame,
a trace over dominions of shadows
and memory rescuing and singing.

It is in this winter
that a resurrection of leaves arrives,
time happens
gazing over icy mirrors,
malevolent and beautiful season,

claro de luna
meciéndose sobre la ingratitud del frío.

Estación de silencio recostado sobre la fuga del tiempo,
estación que apresura los sentidos
que busca el regreso al corazón de la noche
a las paredes como cenizas
a las paredes que escuchan las ofrendas de los vivos
y el caminar de los muertos.

Es en este invierno cuando siento el aleluya de la vida
tu cuerpo escarchado y lleno de los más remotos perfumes.
Espero la fugacidad de la noche y te llamo,
la luz llena y plenaria como una fiesta en su inmensidad,
y así nosotros enmudecimos,
soñamos así con la belleza
somos los mercaderes de la noche,
los viajeros de la noche,
el perpetuo ritmo de una pasión desbordada entre
los hielos,
invierno,
un puerto seguro y entre silencios.

moonlight
swaying over cold ingratitude.

Season of silence leaning on fugitive time,
season that hastens the senses
searching for the return to the heart of the night,
to walls like ashes,
walls that listen to the offerings of the living
and walks of the dead.

It is in this winter when I feel the joy of life,
your body frosted and filled with the remotest of perfumes.
I wait for the brevity of night and call you,
the light is full and complete like a celebration in its immensity,
and thus we become mute,
we dream with beauty,
we are nocturnal merchants,
nocturnal travelers,
perpetual rhythm of an overflowing passion
among ice,
winter,
a safe harbor among silences.

L.N.

THREADS OF HOPE

QUERERES

Jamás pretendí el ascenso sublime
hacia las amuralladas estirpes del
claustro bibliotecal.
Tampoco a ser una de ellos: precisa y sin pausas
cauta en la ortografía, en el humo y en el alcohol.

No quise la fama solapada en una solapa de epitafios profesionales
en esos rótulos de incógnita Poetisa notable, poetisa locuaz.

Sólo quise llegar a ti Cenicienta feucha,
sin reírme de tus pies desgraciadamente inmensos.
Sólo quise llegar a ti Manuel,
sin juzgar las andanzas de tu noche
y tus ojos
que esperan ser recogidos
en una neblina mústia y azul.

Nunca quise reírme de nadie, porque ni lector pretendí,
sólo uno que otro amigo
que por aburrimiento pero jamás por deber
decidió mientras esperaba el tren
leer estos versos.

WISHES

I never tried to make the sublime ascent
toward the forefathers walled up in the
cloistered library.
Nor to be one of them: precise and without pauses
cautious in matters of spelling, smoke and alcohol.

I didn't want the fake fame of fallacious epitaphs profesionals use
in those labels for the incognita noteworthy poetess, loquacious poetess.

I only wanted to reach you homely Cinderella
without laughing at your sadly vast feet.
I only wanted to reach you Manuel
without criticizing your nightly
comings-and-goings and your eyes
waiting to be gathered up
in a blue and gloomy fog.

I never wanted to make fun of anybody, never even went after readers,
just one or two friends
who out of boredom but never out of duty
would decide while waiting for the train
to read these verses.

C.F.

CASTAÑAS EN EL AIRE

En mi paladar,
encontré una
castaña
gozosa, aromática,
como los buenos augurios.

Me hacía cosquillas
en los labios
que se curvaban cuando
sabiamente,
la mordía,
guiñándole
un ojito.

Nadie nos miraba
sólo el cielo colorido,
y nosotras,
éramos madejas doradas,
latiendo en las arterias
del delicioso mordisco.

La castaña y yo
nos columpiábamos
en la tibieza de la boca,
en el vaivén del paladar
en las fogatas
del deseo.

CHESNUTS IN THE AIR

On my palate
I found a
chestnut,
tasty, smelling good
like lucky signs.

It tickled
my lips
they couldn't keep from smiling when
sagely
I bit into it,
throwing it
a wink.

Nobody was watching us
only the high bright sky
and we
were golden tangles
throbbing in the bloodstream
of the savory morsel.

The chestnut and I were swinging
back and forth
in the mouth's warm inside,
in the to and fro of the palate
in the bonfires
of desire.

SEMEJANZAS

Desnudos, ya no nos
parecemos
ni a la muerte
ni al deseo.
Somos más bien, dos
ríos, dos peces detrás
de la sombra,
dos lagartijas
encrispadas
por un sol adormecido
en la niebla.

Desnudos nos parecemos
a los animales
en reposo.
O a la escritura de los niños,
que no pretende más que el sueño,
más que ser cuerpo en las nieblas
o en el silencio
de una misma sangre.

RESEMBLANCES

Naked, we
resemble
neither death
nor desire.
We are, instead, two
rivers, two fish behind
the shadow,
two lizards
clenched
by a sun lulled drowsy
in the mist.

Naked we resemble
animals
at rest.
Or children's writing
seeking only sleep,
to be a body in the mists
or in the silence
of a common blood.

N.L.

¿Cuántas veces yo converso con mis muertos?
Y sus manos, son una textura hundida, y les pregunto cosas
y sus rostros son una memoria de llagas, y la noche
amenazándonos en su caída intempestuosa, pero yo converso con
mis muertos que a lo mejor son tuyos, y los cubro, los empapo
de mi sentir callado y de mis ojos parecidos a los alambres de la
sombra. Siempre me despido de ese cuerpo,
de esos ojos que me parecen un río
de silencio.
Y así aprendo a decirles cosas,
a prometerles un jardín floreciente, florido,
una historia, un nacimiento, una promesa,
y es tan increíble como yo amo a este muerto, que no es mi muerto,
que tampoco es un cadáver. Es un salto de agua, un diálogo,
una costa para cruzar.

How many times do I talk with my dead?
And their hands are rough and wrinkled, and I ask them
things and their faces are a memory of sorrows, and the night
threatens us in its tempestuous fall, but I talk with
my dead which perhaps are yours, and I cover them, saturate
them with my silent sorrow and with my tear-drenched eyes.
I always bid farewell to that body,
to those eyes that seem like a river
of silence.
And this is how I learn to tell them things,
to promise them a blossoming, flowery garden,
a history, a beginning, a promise,
and it is so incredible how I love this dead one, who is not mine,
who is not a cadaver either, but a waterfall, a dialogue,
a shore to be crossed.

LAS MADRES DE LOS PRESOS POLÍTICOS

Las madres de los presos políticos
no se endurecen ni llevan en sus
rostros las huellas y trazos del dolor
las mujeres de los presos
políticos llevan el pan de la victoria
cuando se acercan por las rendijas aterradoras del vacío
y cuando reparten pan, maíz, y sol,
la cárcel se llena de pájaros y brazos cantores
las mujeres de los presos políticos
no lloran cuando se despiden
de los maridos condenados a muerte
de los recientemente torturados
ellas cantan un himno parecido
a los diluvios o a los profundos arco iris
de las delicias
y se van
marchando
y entre sus faldas
germinan niños
y en vez de incendios y lápidas
se repiten como los ríos y la vida
y no son nada de parecidas
a los tacones solapados de
la muerte.

MOTHERS OF POLITICAL PRISONERS

Mothers of political prisoners
do not get hardhearted, nor do they carry in their
faces traces and outlines of pain.
Women of political prisoners
carry victory bread
when they approach the terrifying cracks of the void
and when they hand out bread, corn, and sunshine,
the prison fills up with birds and singing arms.
Women of political prisoners
don't cry when they bid farewell
to their spouses condemned to death,
to the recently tortured.
They sing a hymn that resembles
floods or deep rainbows
of delight
and they leave
marching
and between their skirts
sprout children
and instead of fires and gravestones
they repeat themselves like rivers and life
and they don't seem anything
like the furtive heels of
death.

C.K.C.

JERUSALÉN

Jerusalén,
ciudad con el
corazón
rebanado,
ciudad de vientos,
presagios y azares.
¿Cómo guardarte
en mis manos?
¿Recoger
tus casas de murallas blanqueadas?
¿tus minerales?
¿tus párpados insomniados
para que no te quemen,
para que los hombres necios
gocen de tus brazos
de tus silencios
de aquella sabiduría
sumida
en la agonía de
los tiempos de reina?

Oh Jerusalén,
yo te invoco,
repito tu nombre:
enmudezco
ante el esplendor
de tu silencio
y en tus cúpulas
escribo,
los sueños de la paz.

JERUSALEM

Jerusalem,
city with her
heart
slashed,
city of winds,
omens and misfortune:
how do I hold you
in my hands?
How do I take in your houses, their whitewashed walls?
Your minerals?
Your insomniac eyelids
so that they won't burn you,
so that ignorant men
may delight in your arms,
in your silences,
in that wisdom
buried
under the agony of
these imperious times?

O Jerusalem,
I invoke you,
I repeat your name:
I become speechless
before the splendor
of your silence and on your cupolas
I write
dreams of peace.

R.S.

RACHEL CARSON

I.

En el claro del bosque,
en la redondez ágil de la luz
te encuentras fosforescente
como la más audaz y quieta hoja,
como los sueños de las luciérnagas.
Guardiana del tiempo,
nombradora del agua y de los ríos secos
en tus manos conservas
los gestos más inmensos
los latidos del viento
la lozana mirada de la perseverancia.

II.

Amiga de los pájaros,
del silencio de todos los bosques,
eres un trozo de agua viva,
la cadencia más perpetua
en esa inmensidad de las calles.
guardiana de los secretos,
respetuosa como lo más infinito
que es sublime.

III.

Eres mujer,
plena, jubilosa
asombrada y sencilla.
Tu mano es como un anillo
mientras tocas
las cortezas
de la tierra.

RACHEL CARSON

I.

In the forest's clearing,
in the agile roundness of light
you are fluorescent
like a bold and quiet leaf,
like the dreams of fireflies.
Guardian of time,
namer of water and dry rivers,
in your hands you carry
the immense gestures
the beating of the wind
the pure gaze of perseverance.

II.

Friend of birds,
of the silence of all forests,
you are a fragment of living water,
the most perpetual cadence
in those immense streets,
guardian of secrets,
respectful like the infinite
which is sublime.

III.

You are a woman
full, joyful
surprised and simple.
Your hand is like a ring
sliding over
the bark
of the earth.

IV

Sospechaste de los mercaderes,
de los falsos emperadores.
predijiste sus infamias,
los árboles del Brasil,
las pájaras errabundas de Bengala
y sólo pediste
un tiempo para habitarse.

IV.

You suspected the merchants
to be false emperors,
you predicted their infamies,
the trees of Brazil,
the errant birds of Bengal
and you only asked
for a time to inhabit yourself.

HACEDORA DE PALABRAS

Arqueada
se inclina descalza
por las tintas azules como
mareas de estrellas
y en un preciso y vago
instante,
en la diafanidad del aliento,
elige las palabras.
Las escoge como si fueran
los atuendos más fragantes
de los exquisitos mercados al sur de la tierra,
como si fueran las maderas ágiles,
el alimento frondoso.
Sólo entonces
las acomoda como si salieran del vientre mismo
o de la noche o de sus ojos o del viento que mece
en sus columpios magos,
y ella se deja escribir
entrando al libro sagrado
de su voz.

MAKER OF WORDS

Arched
she bends over barefoot
through blue inks like
tides of stars
in a precise and vague
instant,
in a translucence of breath,
she chooses the words.
She selects them as if they were
the most fragrant attires
from exquisite markets south of the earth,
as if they were agile woods,
leafy delicacies.
Only then
does she arrange them as if they emerged from her belly
or from the night or from her eyes or the wind that rocks
in its magical swing
and she allows herself to be written
entering the sacred book
of her voice.

M.B.G.

CALENDARIOS ABIERTOS

No hay precisos calendarios
en el desierto,
me dijo.
El tiempo es lento,
sin ingratitudes,
indefinido,
como los conjuros.

En el desierto, me dijo
más vale dejarse llevar
por los caprichos de la luz,
por la insinuante danza de la arena humedecida.

Conviene estar atentos
a las ondulaciones del aire,
al cambio del rastro sobre las arenas
ondulantes.

Todo cambia en el desierto:
La luz, el viento descalzo,
las iguanas centelleantes,
las hienas azules,
los visitantes imaginarios.

Todo eso me dijo
mientras su voz ocupaba el horizonte
y yo aprendía a oírla.

OPEN CALENDARS

He told me
there are no precise calendars
in the desert.
Time is slow,
without ungratefulness,
indefinite,
like incantations.

In the desert, he told me,
it was better to let oneself be carried
by the whims of light,
by the insinuating dance of moist sand.

It is best to be alert
to the undulations of air,
to the fluctuating tracks on the undulating
sands.

Everything changes in the desert:
The light, the barefoot wind,
the sparkling iguanas,
the blue hyenas,
the imaginary visitors.

He told me all this
in a voice that occupied the horizon
and I learned to hear it.

GÉNESIS

I.

Por la noche
sobre nuestras cabezas
descienden las estrellas,
hilos sagrados de la noche.

II.

Por la noche,
en este desierto
de Biblias invisibles,
de nómadas y conjuros,
las estrellas nos
cubren
como un libro de rezos.

III.

La luna es una pluma aguda y clarividente
rodeando toda la oscuridad.
Transcurre la noche.
La noche es
tu cuerpo que se aleja,
navega intermitente por las sábanas de agua.
Una almohada desquiciada
divide nuestros cuerpos
que sueñan el sueño de los otros,
a veces el de todos.

IV.

De pronto,
mi cuerpo gira y te rodea
como una cascada de lluvias,
como el principio de los anillos amadores.
Rodeo tu cintura,
una frontera peligrosa.

GENESIS

I.
Over our heads
through the night
the stars descend,
sacred threads of evening.

II.
Through the night
in this desert
of invisible Bibles,
of nomads and incantations,
stars
spread over us
like a book of prayers.

III.
The moon is a sharp and clairvoyant feather
surrounding all obscurity.
Night passes.
Night is
your body that withdraws and
navigates intermittently through sheets of water.
A ruffled pillow
divides our bodies
dreaming the dreams of others
and sometimes those of all.

IV.
Suddenly
my body turns and surrounds you
like a cascade of raindrops,
like the origin of loving rings.
I encircle your waist,
a dangerous frontier.

Nuestras piernas se entrelazan
a través de la noche,
y veo que ese cuerpo envejecido
comienza a aclarar
en mi caricia.

V.

Los cuerpos deciden que
no hay fronteras
como los hombres y mujeres
cansados de la guerra.
Tu rostro ya no se desfigura.
Recupera la salvaje luz del amor.
Cruzo tus labios y tus piernas,
el destino de tu sexo.

VI.

No hay países entre tú y yo.
No hay espacios ajenos.
No escogemos idiomas.
No hay idiomas para
dividirnos.
Tus amigos ya son los míos.
Untamos la boca como
quienes untan el pan o los
trozos de la memoria
que son una sábana grandiosa
y magnifica que nos
protege
del temor a la paz.

VII.

Ya nos reconocemos.
No soy esa extraña de otra patria.
Soy todas las mujeres
rodeando al enemigo que ahora es un conocido

Our legs intertwine
through the night,
and that aging body that I see
becomes clear
in my caress.

V.

The bodies decide
there are no frontiers
like men and women
worn out by war.
Your face is no longer disfigured.
It recovers the savage light of love.
I cross your lips and your legs,
the destiny of your sex.

VI.

There are no countries between you and me.
There are no foreign spaces.
We choose no languages.
No language
can divide us.
Your friends are already mine.
We smear our mouths like
those who butter bread or
fragments of memory
that splendid and
magnificent bedsheet that
protects us
from the fear of peace.

VII.

Now that we recognize each other.
I'm not that stranger from another country.
I'm every woman
surrounding the enemy who is now familiar

y tú amas mi vejez, mis estrías,
mis hijos que son los tuyos
y que no debes matar.

VIII.

Esta noche
hemos visitado otras
historias.
Tus sueños ya no
son los de los hombres
mutilados.
Yo no soy la niña del Salvador
sin piernas,
ni la judía con los tatuajes del espanto.
Hemos derribado a la guerra
con un beso victorioso
y en la oscuridad de esta noche
no pensamos claros
sumergidos en el sueño blanco de la paz.

and you love my old age, my lines,
my children who are yours
and whom you must not kill.

VIII.

Tonight
we have visited other
histories.
Your dreams are no longer
those of mutilated
men.
I am not the girl from El Salvador
without legs
nor the Jew with tattoos of terror.
We have demolished war
with a victorious kiss
and in this dark night
we don't think clearly
immersed in this white dream of peace.

C.K.C.

The Author

Marjorie Agosín is a native of Chile who now lives in Wellesley, Massachusetts, where she is a professor of Latin American Literature at Wellesley College. Much of her work focuses on the human rights abuses that have taken place in her native country and in other regions throughout the world. She has been honored with the Henrietta Zold Award from Hadassah (2002), with the United Nations Leadership Award on Human Rights (1998) and with the Jeanette Rankin (1995) and Good Neighbor Awards (1990). As a poet, anthologist and writer of short prose, she has also received wide critical acclaim. In 1995 she received the Latino Literature Prize for *Hacia la ciudad espléndida* and subsequently, the Letras de Oro prize for *Noche estrellada*. For the documentary based on her book, *Scraps of Life: The Chilean Arpilleras*, she was recognized with the distinguished Peabody Award for Best Documentary (1992). Among her most recent volumes are: *A Map of Hope: Women's Writing on Human Rights*, *To Mend the World: Women Respond to 9/11* and *The Angel of Memory*.

Marjorie Agosín has traveled extensively and she has been a visiting artist and scholar at several universities in the U.S. and abroad, including the University of Los Andes, the University of Georgia and Barnard College. This publication honors her contributions to Latino Literature in the United States and to Latin American Letters.

THE EDITOR AND THE TRANSLATORS

NOTE: TRANSLATORS ARE IDENTIFIED BY INITIALS
AFTER EACH POEM, OR GROUP OF POEMS, SHE/HE TRANSLATED.

CELESTE KOSTOPULOS-COOPERMAN is the author of *The Lyrical Vision of María Luisa Bombal*, (Tamesis Press, London 1988). Her publications range from collections of literary essays on well-known Latin American authors to entries in critical editions show-casing the work of women authors. Her translations have appeared in such distinguished journals as *Agni, The American Voice, Harpers, Human Rights Quarterly* and *The Michigan Quarterly Review*. She was recognized by the American Literary Translators' Association for her translation of *Circles of Madness* (M. Agosín, White Pine Press, 1992), a book dedicated to the Mothers of the Plaza de Mayo and sponsored by Amnesty International. Among her translations of the work of Marjorie Agosín are: *Tapestries of Hope/Threads of Love: The Arpillera Movement in Chile 1974-1994 , A Cross and A Star: Memoirs of a Jewish Girl in Chile*, both by the University of New Mexico Press, *Always from Somewhere Else/A Memoir of My Jewish Father* (The Feminist Press, New York), *Rain in the Desert* (Sherman Asher Publishing, New Mexico) and *An Absence of Shadows* (White Pine Press, New York). She is professor of Humanities and Modern Languages and directs the Latin American Studies Program at Suffolk University, Boston, Massachusetts.

MARY BERG is a lecturer in the Harvard Extension Program and at M.I.T. She has published extensively on Latin American authors, with a particular interest in women's fiction. Among her translated works are a Peruvian novel by Laura Riesco (*Ximena at the Crossroads*, 1998), an Argentine novel by Libertad Demitropulos *(River of Sorrows, 2000)* and the first volume in the Brandeis series of Jewish Women, *Uncertain Travelers: Conversations with Jewish Immigrants to America* by Marjorie Agosín (1999).

MÓNICA BRUNO GALMOZZI was born in Costa Rica of Italian parents. She works as a Spanish interpreter at Shriners Burns Hospital for Children in Boston. She began working with Marjorie Agosín in 1988, while she pursued her B.A. at Wellesley College. Among Ms. Bruno's translations of Marjorie Agosín are the books *Melodious Women* and *The Council of the Fairies*, as well as the performance piece "Tres Vidas" performed by CORE Ensemble.

COLA FRANZEN has published translations of poetry, fiction and criticism by Spanish and Latin Ameriican authors. Among these are Claudio Guillén, Saúl Yurkievich and Gerardo Mosquera. Winner of The Harold Morton Landon Translation Award in 2000 for her translation of Jorge Guillén's *Horses in the Air* (City Lights, 1999), her most recent publications include *Dreams of the Abandoned Seducer*, a novel (University of Nebraska Press, 1998) and a book of poems, *The Collapsible Couple*, by the Argentine writer, Alicia Borinsky.

NAOMI LINDSTROM is professor of Spanish and Portuguese at the University of Texas at Austin and Vice President of the Latin American Jewish Studies Association. Among her recent publications are: *Twentieth Century Spanish American Fiction, Jewish Issues in Argentine Literature, Jorge Luis Borges: A Study of the Short Fiction* and *The Social Conscience of Latin American Writing*.

LAURA NAKAZAWA has translated several works by Marjorie Agosín, among them *The Angel of Memory*, and other collections of poems. A native of Uruguay, she has over eighteen years of experience in the field of translation and interpretation. She lives in Wellesley, Massachusetts, with her husband and their three daughters.

RICHARD SCHAAF is a translator of contemporary Latin American poets, among them Roque Dalton and Cristina Peri Rossi. He is former editor of Azul Editions, which published works of contemporary poets in translation. He lives with his wife and child in Falls Church, Virginia.

A SELECTED BIBLIOGRAPHY
OF WORK BY MARJORIE AGOSÍN

POETRY

Conchali. New York, N.Y.: Senda Nueva de Ediciones, 1980.

Brujas y algo más/Witches and Other Things. Translated by Cola Franzen, Pittsburgh: Latin American Literary Review Press, 1984. Second print ing, with a prologue by Elena Poniatowska. Pittsburgh: Latin American Literary Review Press, 1986.

Las zonas del dolor/Zones of Pain. Translated by Cola Franzen. Fredonia, New York: White Pine Press, 1988. Finalist, *Los Angeles Times* Book Award

Hogueras. Santiago, Chile: Editorial Universitaria, 1986.

Hogueras/Bonfires. Translated by Naomi Lindstrom. Arizona: Bilingual Press, 1990.

Travesías generosas/Generous Journeys. Translated by Cola Franzen. University of Nevada, Reno: The Black Rock Press, 1992.

Círculos de locura: Madres de la Plaza de Mayo/Circles of Madness: Mothers of the Plaza de Mayo. Translated by Celeste Kostopulos-Cooperman. Fredonia, New York: White Pine Press, 1992. Winner of the ALTA Prize for Poetry in Translation.

Sargazo. Buenos Aires: Editorial Carlos Lohlé, 1991.

Sargazo/Sargasso. Translated by Cola Franzen. Fredonia, New York: White Pine Press, 1993.

Hacia la ciudad espléndida/Toward the Splendid City. Translated by Richard Schaaf. Arizona: Bilingual Press, 1994. Winner of the 1995 Latino Literature Prize.

Querida Ana Frank/Dear Anne Frank. Translated by Richard Schaaf. Washington D.C.: Azul Editions, 1994. Reprinted with additional poems translated by Cola Franzen and Mónica Bruno by The University Press of New England, Brandeis Series on European Jewry, 1998.

Noche estrellada/Starry Night. Translated by Mary Berg. Santiago, Chile/Fredonia, New York, LOM Ediciones/White Pine Press, 1996). Winner of the Letras de Oro Prize for Poetry.

Mujeres melodiosas/Melodious Women. Translated by Monica Bruno Galmozzi, Pittsburgh: Latin American Literary Review Press, 1997.

El consejo de las hadas/Council of the Fairies. Translated by Monica Bruno Galmozzi

with a prologue by Elena Poniatowska Washington, D.C., Azul
Editions, 1997.

Las chicas desobedientes. Madrid: Torremozas, 1997.

Una ausencia de sombras/An Absence of Shadows. Translated by Celeste Kostopulos-
Cooperman, Cola Franzen and Mary Berg. Buffalo, New York: White
Pine Press, 1998.

Lluvia en el desierto/Rain in the Desert. Translated by Celeste Kostopulos-
Cooperman. Santa Fe, New Mexico: Sherman Asher Publishing, 1999.
Honorable Mention *Forward Magazine.*

The Angel of Memory. Translated by Laura Nakazawa, San Antonio, Texas: Wings
Press, 2002.

MEMOIRS

The Alphabet in My Hands. Translated by Nancy Abraham Hall. N.J.: Rutgers
University Press, 1999.

Amigas. With Emma Sepúlveda . Austin: University of Texas Press, 2000.

Always from Somewhere Else. A Memoir of My Chilean Jewish Father. Translated by
Celeste Kostopulos-Cooperman with an introduction by Elizabeth Rosa
Horan. N.Y.: The Feminist Press, 1998.

A Cross and a Star: Memoirs of a Jewish Girl in Chile. Translated with an intro-
duction by Celeste Kostopulos-Cooperman. University of New Mexico
Press, 1995.

A Cross and a Star: Memoirs of a Jewish Girl in Chile. United Kingdom: Gardner
Press, 1997.

A Cross and a Star: Memoirs of a Jewish Girl in Chile. Translated by Celeste
Kostopulos-Cooperman with an introduction by Laura Riesco, (paper
back edition). N.Y.: The Feminist Press, 1997.

Sagrada memoria: reminiscencias de una niña judía en Chile. Santiago, Chile:
Editorial Cuarto Propio, 1994.

EDITED ANTHOLOGIES

To Mend the World: Women Respond to 9/11. With Betty Jean Craige. Buffalo,
N.Y.: White Pine Press, 2002.

Taking Root. Ohio University Press, 2002.

Uncertain Travelers: Jewish Women Emigrants to the Americas. Hanover, N.H.:
University Press of New England, 1999.

The House of Memory: Stories by Jewish Women Writers of Latin America. Translation
editor, Elizabeth Rosa Horan; stories translated by Roberta Gordenstein
et al. New York, N.Y.: The Feminist Press, 1999.

*A Map of Hope: Women Writing on Human Rights–an International Literary
Anthology.* New Brunswick, N.J.: Rutgers University Press, 1999.

A Map of Hope. United Kingdom: Penguin Books, 1999.

A Necklace of Words: Mexican Women Writers. With Nancy Abraham Hall,
Fredonia, N.Y.: White Pine Press, 1997.

Magical Sites: Women Travelers to the Americas. With Julie Leveson, Fredonia, N.Y.:
White Pine Press, 1997.

A Dream of Light and Shadow: Portraits of Latin American Women Writers.
Albuquerque: University of New Mexico Press, 1996.

Gabriela Mistral. Santiago, Chile: Pontificia Universidad Catolica de Chile, 1996.

What is Secret: An Anthology of Chilean Women Writers. Fredonia, N.Y.: White
Pine Press, 1995.

These Are Not Sweet Girls: 20th Century Latin American Women Poets. Fredonia,
N.Y.: White Pine Press, 1993. Reprinted 2002.

A Gabriela Mistral Reader. Translated by Maria Giachetti. Fredonia, N.Y.: White
Pine Press, 1993.

Chilean FolkTales Retold. With Celeste Kostopulos-Cooperman, Stratford, Ont.:
Williams-Wallace, 1992.

Secret Weavers: Women and Fantastic Literature in Latin America. With an
Afterword by Celeste Kostopulos-Cooperman, Fredonia, N.Y.: White
Pine Press, 1991; Spanish Edition, February 1993.

Landscapes of a New Land: Short Stories by Latin American Women Writers.
Fredonia, N.Y.: White Pine Press, 1989. Reprinted 1993.

Visions and Revisions: Latin American Women Poets. With Cola Franzen.
Peterborough, England: Spectacular Diseases Press, 1987.

María Luisa Bombal: Critical Essays. With Elena Gascón-Vera and Joy Renjilian-
Burgy, Tempe, Arizona: Bilingual Review Press, 1987.

BOOKS OF LITERARY CRITICISM

The Invisible Dreamer: Memory, Judaism and Human Rights. Santa Fe, New Mexico: Sherman Asher, 2001.

Passion, Memory, and Identity: Twentieth-Century Latin American Jewish Women Writers. Albuquerque, N.M.: University of New Mexico Press, 1999.

A Woman's Gaze: Latin American Women Artists. Fredonia, N.Y.: White Pine Press, 1998.

Tapestries of Hope, Threads of Love: The Arpillera Movement in Chile, 1974-1994. Translated by Celeste Kostopulos-Cooperman with a Foreword by Isabel Allende, Albuquerque, N.M.: University of New Mexico Press, 1996.

Ashes of Revolt: Essays on Human Rights. Fredonia, N.Y.: White Pine Press, 1996.

Hay Otra Voz: Essays on Hispanic Women Poets. With Emma Sepúlveda, Puerto Rico: Ediciones Maerena, 1995.

Surviving Beyond Fear: Women, Children and Human Rights in Latin America. Fredonia, N. Y.: White Pine Press, 1993.

Las hacedoras: Mujer, Imagen y Escritura. Santiago, Chile: Cuarto Propio, 1993.

Literatura fantástica del Cono Sur: Las Mujeres. San José, Costa Rica: EDUCA, 1992.

Violeta Parra, o la expresión inefable: un análisis crítico de su poesía, prosa, y pintura. With Inés Dolz Blackburn. Santiago, Chile: Planeta, 1992.

Violeta Parra, santa de pura greda: un estudio de su obra poética. With Inés Dolz Blackburn. Santiago, Chile: Planeta, 1991

René Eppelbaum and the Mothers of the Plaza de Mayo. Toronto, Canada: Williams Wallace, 1989; Trenton, N.J.: Red Sea Press, 1990.

Literatura y derechos humanos en Latinoamérica. San José, Costa Rica: EDUCA, 1989.

Women of Smoke/Mujeres de humo. Translated by Naomi Lindstrom. Pittsburgh, Pennsylvania: Latin American Literary Review Press, 1988.

Scraps of Life: Chilean arpilleras: Chilean Women and the Pinochet Dictatorship. Translated by Cola Franzen. Trenton, N.J.: Red Sea Press, 1987. Reprinted, 1989. Also translated into German, 1990.

Silencio e imaginación: metáforas de la escritura femenina. Mexico City: Katún, 1986.

Pablo Neruda. Translated by Lorraine Roses, Boston, MA: G.K. Hall (Twayne series), 1986.

Edited by Marjorie Agosín & Betty Jean Craige

To Mend the World
Women Reflect on 9/11

The first collection of its kind, this volume gives women from different ethnic and cultural backgrounds a space in which to reflect on the tragic events of September 11, 2001, as well as on the political climate and U.S. image in the world both preceding and after the attack on the United States. Their essays create a multi-dimensional image both poignant and provocative.

Included are Mahnaz Afkhami, Jessica Lampert, Julia Alvarez, Diana Zykofsky Anhalt, Claudia Bernardi, Elise Boulding, Alida Brill, Lori Marie Carlson, Aviva Chomsky, Judith Otrtiz Cofer, Carol Dine, Judy Dworin, Farideh Dayanim Goldin, Patricia Greene, Luisa Igloria, Alexandra Johnson, Rebecca Leavitt, Brigid Aileen Milligan, Toni Morrison, Laura Rocha Nakazawa, Mirta Ojito, Margarita Papandreou, Margaret Randall, Emma Sepúlveda, Ruth Knafo Setton, Bapsi Sidhwa, Judith A. Sokoloff, and Jane G. Stapleton.

240 pages $17.95

THE SECRET WEAVERS SERIES

Series General Editor: Marjorie Agosín

Dedicated to bringing the rich and varied writing
by Latin American women to the English-speaking audience.

Volume 3
LANDSCAPES OF A NEW LAND
Short Fiction by Latin American Women
194 pages $12.00

Volume 1
ALFONSINA STORNI: SELECTED POEMS
Edited by Marion Freeman
72 pages $8.00 paper

OTHER LATIN AMERICAN TITLES

THERE IS NO ROAD
Proverbs by Antonia Machado
128 pages $14.00

IN THIS SACRED PLACE
A novel by Poli Delano
240 pages $16.00

A WOMAN'S GAZE: LATIN AMERICAN WOMEN ARTISTS
Edited by Marjorie Agosín
264 PAGES $20.00

AN ABSENCE OF SHADOWS
Poems on Human Rights by Marjorie Agosín
212 pages $15.00

WINDOWS THAT OPEN INWARD:
POEMS BY PABLO NERUDA PHOTOGRAPHS BY MILTON ROGOVIN
Translated by Bly, Maloney, Merwin, O'Daly, Reid, Vega, Wright
96 pages $20.00

ISLA NEGRA
POEMS BY PABLO NERUDA PHOTOGRAPHS BY MILTON ROGOVIN
Translated by Jacketti, Maloney & Zlotchew
96 pages $12.00

STARRY NIGHT
Poems by Marjorie Agosín
Translated by Mary G. Berg
96 pages $12.00

ASHES OF REVOLT
Essays by Marjorie Agosín
128 pages $13.00

SARGASSO
Poems by Marjorie Agosín
Translated by Cola Franzen
92 pages $12.00   Bilingual

SELECTED POEMS OF MIGUAL HERNÁNDEZ
Translated by Robert Bly, Timothy Baland, Hardi St Martin and James Wright
138 pages $11.00   Bilingual

ABOUT WHITE PINE PRESS

Established in 1973, White Pine Press is a non-profit publishing house dedicated to enriching our literary heritage; promoting cultural awareness, understanding, and respect; and, through literature, addressing social and human rights issues. This mission is accomplished by discovering, producing, and marketing to a diverse circle of readers exceptional works of poetry, fiction, non-fiction, and literature in translation from around the world. Through White Pine Press, authors' voices reach out across cultural, ethnic, and gender boundaries to educate and to entertain.

To insure that these voices are heard as widely as possible, White Pine Press arranges author reading tours and speaking engagements at various colleges, universities, organizations, and bookstores throughout the country. White Pine Press works with colleges and public schools to enrich curricula and promotes discussion in the media. Through these efforts, literature extends beyond the books to make a difference in a rapidly changing world.

As a non-profit organization, White Pine Press depends on support from individuals, foundations, and government agencies to bring you important work that would not be published by profit-driven publishing houses. Our grateful thanks to the many individuals who support this effort as Friends of White Pine Press and to the following organizations: Amter Foundation, Ford Foundation, Korean Culture and Arts Foundation, Lannan Foundation, Lila Wallace-Reader's Digest Fund, Margaret L. Wendt Foundation, Mellon Foundation, National Endowment for the Arts, New York State Council on the Arts, Trubar Foundation, Witter Bynner Foundation, the Slovenian Ministry of Culture, The U.S.-Mexico Fund for Culture, and Wellesley College.

Please support White Pine Press' efforts to present voices that promote cultural awareness and increase understanding and respect among diverse populations of the world. Tax-deductible donations can be made to:

White Pine Press
P.O. Box 236, Buffalo, New York 14201

The Tiara Club

For Princess Lisa,
with lots of love, x
VF

for four little princes, Alex, Finlay,
Xavier and Felix
SG

www.tiaraclub.co.uk

ORCHARD BOOKS
338 Euston Road, London NW1 3BH
Orchard Books Australia
Hachette Children's Books
Level 17/207 Kent Street, Sydney, NSW 2000, Australia
A Paperback Original
First published in Great Britain in 2005
Text © copyright Vivian French 2005
Illustrations © copyright Sarah Gibb 2005
The rights of Vivian French and Sarah Gibb to be
identified as the author and illustrator of this work
have been asserted by them in accordance with
the Copyright, Designs and Patents Act, 1988.

A CIP catalogue record for this book is available
from the British Library.
ISBN 978 1 84362 860 6
9 10

Printed in Great Britain

The Tiara Club

Princess Katie
and the Silver Pony

By Vivian French
Illustrated by Sarah Gibb

ORCHARD BOOKS

The Royal Palace Academy
for the Preparation of Perfect Princesses

(Known to our students as '*The Princess Academy*')

OUR SCHOOL MOTTO:
*A Perfect Princess always thinks of others before herself,
and is kind, caring and truthful.*

We offer the complete curriculum for all princesses, including –

How to talk to a Dragon	*Designing and Creating the Perfect Ball Gown*
Creative Cooking for Perfect Palace Parties	*Avoiding Magical Mistakes*
Wishes, and how to use them Wisely	*Descending a Staircase as if Floating on Air*

Our head teacher, Queen Gloriana, is present at all times, and students are well looked after by the school Fairy Godmother.

Visiting tutors and experts include –

KING PERCIVAL (Dragons)	*QUEEN MOTHER MATILDA (Etiquette, Posture and Poise)*
LADY VICTORIA (Banquets)	*THE GRAND HIGH DUCHESS DELIA (Costume)*

We award tiara points to encourage
our princesses towards the next level.
All princesses who win enough points in their
first year are welcomed to the Tiara Club
and presented with a silver tiara.

Tiara Club princesses are invited to return
next year to Silver Towers, our very special
residence for Perfect Princesses, where
they may continue their education
at a higher level.

PLEASE NOTE:
Princesses are expected to arrive at the Academy
with a *minimum* of:

TWENTY BALL GOWNS
(with all necessary hoops,
petticoats, etc)

TWELVE DAY DRESSES

SEVEN GOWNS
suitable for garden parties,
and other special
day occasions

TWELVE TIARAS

DANCING SHOES
five pairs

VELVET SLIPPERS
three pairs

RIDING BOOTS
two pairs

Cloaks, muffs, stoles, gloves
and other essential
accessories as required

How do you do? It's LOVELY to
meet you...we're all so glad you're here!
OH! I'm so silly! Maybe you don't know
who we are? We're the Princesses Katie
(that's me), Charlotte, Emily, Alice, Daisy
and Sophia, and we share the Rose Room
Dormitory at the Princess Academy and
one day we'll ALL be members of the
TOTALLY fabulous Tiara Club! Just as long
as we get enough tiara points, of course.
Do you ever feel really TIRED after
a party? Well, we had a WONDERFUL
Birthday Ball here at the Academy,
but for the next few days it
was SO hard to get up...

Chapter One

I couldn't believe it. The alarm bell was ringing and RINGING! I put my pillow over my head, and shut my eyes tightly.

WHOOMPH! The pillow was snatched away, and there was Princess Alice grinning at me.

"It's no good," she said cheerfully.

"Fairy G's been in twice now, and if we don't get down to breakfast in ten minutes we'll ALL get minus tiara points and NONE of us will ever be members of the Tiara Club!"

"I'm TIRED!" I moaned.

"Cheer up!" Princess Sophia plonked herself down on my bed. "It's Friday today, so tomorrow's Saturday—"

"AND THAT'S THE ROYAL PARADE!" Charlotte and Emily shouted together. Daisy threw her pillow in the air and cheered.

"And we'll all be wearing our very best dresses!" she crowed.

I groaned, and crawled out of bed.

"Eight minutes!" Alice warned me. "DO hurry up, Katie – we simply CAN'T have Rose Room beaten by Princess Perfecta and her creepy crew."

That did make me hurry. In fact, I totally ZOOMED into my clothes. Princess Perfecta ALWAYS likes to be best at everything, and she's a terrible show-off. She was here last year, so she should be a senior, and a member of the Tiara Club, but she didn't get enough tiara points!

So she's back in Year One with us – and that's made her as mean as a snake – at least, that's what Alice's big sister told Alice.

As soon as I was dressed we rushed out of the dormitory and down the winding stairs. We were halfway down when Alice

stopped so suddenly we almost fell on top of her.

"LOOK!" she gasped, and she pointed out of the tower window.

We looked, and we gasped too.

The most beautiful coach any of us had ever seen was standing by the front steps of the academy.

It was shaped like a wonderful pearly seashell, and it was sparkling all over in the sunshine. The seats were covered in softly gleaming white satin cushions, and snow-white furry rugs were heaped everywhere. Six piebald ponies, harnessed with silver bridles and silver reins were in between the shafts, and tiny silver bells tinkled every time they shook their heads.

"It's MAGIC!" I breathed, and we gazed at it in absolute raptures until Sophia said, "Oh NO! Look at the TIME!"

We scraped into breakfast by a whisker. The dining hall is very long, with portraits of amazingly grand and gracious princesses all along the walls. Our teachers sit at the far end on golden thrones, but we sit on benches at long wooden tables, and we actually eat off CHINA plates!

Sophia was SO shocked when she first arrived (she'd absolutely NEVER eaten off anything except gold), but Charlotte pointed out the food would taste the same, so she didn't make a fuss.

Because we were so late we had to sit on the end table, and there were Perfecta and Floreen.

"Oh goodness me," Perfecta sneered, looking at Emily and Daisy's bird's nest hair. "I can see what kind of wish YOU'LL be making this morning. YOU'LL be wishing for a hairbrush!" And she and Floreen fell about as if she'd made the best joke ever.

"Ignore her!" Sophia hissed under her breath, but Emily was looking at Perfecta with wide eyes.

"What do you mean?" she asked. "What wish?"

"WHAT?" Perfecta threw up her hands as if Emily had asked her something really stupid.

"You mean, you don't KNOW?" She sniggered loudly. "It's WISH CLASS this morning." She turned to Floreen as they got up from the table. "Don't you think it's QUITE extraordinary that Queen Gloriana lets such silly princesses through the door?"

Chapter Two

Just as I was finishing my breakfast Queen Gloriana came sailing into the dining hall. She's our headmistress, and she's wonderfully tall and graceful. She's also a little bit scary, because she expects us to be PERFECT princesses...and sometimes that can be very hard work.

I was pleased to see Fairy G stomping in behind her. Fairy G's much more fun; she's the school's Fairy Godmother, and she keeps an eye on all of us.

"Good morning, my dear young princesses," Queen Gloriana said, and paused while we made our curtsies.

I didn't do too badly, but Charlotte wobbled madly and clutched at the table. A butter dish crashed onto the floor, and of course EVERYBODY turned and stared. Charlotte blushed bright red, and Perfecta and Floreen sniggered.

Queen Gloriana went on speaking as if nothing had happened. "As you know, princesses, tomorrow is the Royal Parade, and this year there will be something a little special. Our good friend King Constantin of Forever and Faraway has been kind enough to present the school with a very beautiful coach. I have decided that the princess who has the most tiara points by the end of today will ride in the Seashell Coach, and lead the Parade!"

Immediately there was a burst of whispering. Imagine riding in that GORGEOUS coach!

Tap tap! Fairy G tapped a chair.
"Time for all first years to go to
Wish Class! Follow me!"

"Wow!" Alice whispered in my ear. "Do you think we can wish for anything we want?" Her eyes were dancing, and I began to feel excited as I followed Sophia and Emily out into the long black and white marble corridor that

led to the classrooms. Daisy and Charlotte were right behind, and so were Perfecta and Floreen.

"I know SOMEONE who needs to wish she can curtsey properly," Floreen said spitefully as we hurried after Fairy G.

The classroom wasn't at all grand, except for a beautiful sparkly chandelier that glittered in the light. The four tables were just plain wood, and the chairs weren't covered in satin or anything like that – although they did have soft red velvet cushions. Charlotte, Sophia, Emily, Daisy, Alice and I managed to get a table to ourselves.

I couldn't help grinning when I saw the other princesses trying to avoid having Perfecta and Floreen sit with them.

"NOW – LISTEN CAREFULLY!" Fairy G boomed at us. She's very big, and her voice is really loud. "YOU WILL EACH HAVE ONE WISH, AND ONE ONLY. THINK HARD, AND THEN WRITE IT DOWN. REMEMBER, ONCE IT'S WRITTEN DOWN IT CAN'T BE CHANGED."

She fished in her pocket, brought out a huge alarm clock, and banged it down on her desk.

"YOU HAVE FIVE MINUTES! BEGIN!"

At once we could hear murmurings from the other tables.

31

Princess Freya called out, "Please, Fairy G, are we meant to be thinking of something princessy? Or can we wish for whatever we want?"

Fairy G smiled a mysterious sort of smile. "That's for me to know, and you to find out," she said.

"Oh." Freya looked puzzled. "So can I wish for a kitten?"

Fairy G didn't answer. Princess Perfecta snorted loudly.

"REALLY!" she sniffed. "Fancy wanting a KITTEN!"

"That's right," Floreen agreed. "Some princesses are SO babyish."

"I don't see anything wrong with wanting a kitten," I said loudly. I was fed up with Perfecta.

"I'D like..." my mind whirled, and I thought of the Seashell Coach – "...a pony!"

I had a sudden idea. The piebald ponies pulling the coach had been pretty, but somehow not quite right...and I knew what would be EXACTLY PERFECT!

"A SILVER pony!"

"OOOOH!" Beside me Emily's eyes lit up.

"That's BRILLIANT, Katie!" said Charlotte.

"Wouldn't it be sweet?" sighed Sophia and Daisy.

"Just imagine!" Alice said. "A silver pony. We could feed it sugar lumps..."

"Well," I said slowly, "I was more thinking of—"

"TIME'S UP!" boomed Fairy G. "I'm coming round to collect your wishes NOW!"

We looked at each other.

"So shall we?" Charlotte whispered. "Shall we wish for a silver pony? One each?"

"YES!" I said, much too loudly. I saw Perfecta glare at me. "SIX silver ponies – to pull the Seashell Coach! They'd be GORGEOUS!"

And we all scribbled madly as Fairy G stamped up to our table.

Chapter Three

Nothing happened. There was
no sign of any magic. Fairy G
went back to her desk, and
sorted through the pieces of
paper.

"H'm," she said. "Very creative.
And now for your tiara points."

We all sat up sharply. Tiara
points?

"That's right." Fairy G gave us an odd kind of smile. "Queen Gloriana has asked me to give a hundred tiara points to the princess who has asked for the most thoughtful and unselfish wish."

I could feel my eyes popping out of my head. A HUNDRED POINTS!!! That would mean—

"Exactly!" Fairy G knew what I was thinking – me, and every other princess in the class. "A hundred points will earn you a place in the Seashell Coach!"

"But that's not fair!" Princess Eglantine was bright red in the face. She was a friend of Perfecta's – at least, she was when Perfecta allowed her to be. "That's SO not fair! I'd NEVER have wished for curly blonde hair if I'd known that!"

Have I told you that Fairy G is BIG? Well, when Eglantine said that she grew ENORMOUS!

And she looked so scary I would have dived under the table if I hadn't been too frightened to move.

"Princess Eglantine," Fairy G roared, "you will take twenty MINUS tiara points! NO Princess worthy of the name should EVER speak the way you have just spoken!"

Eglantine cowered in her seat, and whispered "Sorry, Fairy G."

"HARRRUMPH!" Fairy G still looked angry, but she shrank back to her usual size. "Let me remind you ALL that a Perfect Princess should not EVER need to be told to think of others before herself."

I began to feel nervous; what would Fairy G think about our silver ponies? Would she give us minus tiara points too?

"Now," Fairy G said firmly, "it's time to announce the winner. Are you ready?"

We sat up, folded our hands in our laps, and nodded. I could feel my heart pitter-pattering in my chest, even though I knew I couldn't possibly win.

"And the winner is..." Fairy G stopped for a dramatic pause.

We held our breath.

"And the winner is...PRINCESS PERFECTA!"

There was a long silence. I could see Perfecta smiling a cat-that's-got-the-cream type smile.

"Princess Perfecta, please read your winning wish out to the class," Fairy G said, handing Perfecta back her piece of paper.

Perfecta stood up.

"I wish, not for a perfect face, but truthful heart, and perfect grace," she said in a sing-song voice.

Beside me Alice gasped loudly.

"What is it?" I whispered.

"She's a CHEAT!" she hissed.

"SILENCE!" boomed Fairy G, but it was so odd! She gave Alice a sly little wink!

"And now, class dismissed! Your wishes will be waiting for you in the Great Hall," Fairy G went on. She smiled a HUGE smile at Perfecta. "And I'm sure we ALL wish you well, Princess Perfecta – and DO enjoy your wish, and your ride in the Seashell Coach."

We scrambled out of the classroom. We tried hard to walk properly down the long corridor that led to the Great Hall, but at the same time we were DYING to get there as fast as we could.

Would there really be six silver ponies waiting for us? I couldn't wait!

As we scooted along Alice was positively exploding with rage. "Perfecta SO cheated!" she said. "That was my SISTER'S wish last year! Why on EARTH didn't Fairy G say something?"

I was remembering Fairy G's little wink. "I think Fairy G's up to something," I said, and then we were at the door of the Great Hall.

It was AMAZING.

Chapter Four

You know when it's a sunny
day, and little golden sparkles
of dust float in the sunbeams?
Well, the Hall was FULL of
sparkles just like that, only
much MUCH sparklier. Most
of our class were already there,
and we could see princesses
spinning round and round in

fantastic ball gowns, or dancing like ballerinas.

Lisa and Jemima were singing like nightingales. Nancy was walking up and down on stilts. Freya was stroking a fluffy kitten. It was SO incredible! And up at the far end Queen Gloriana was talking to Fairy G, and some of the other teachers.

Eglantine, Floreen and Perfecta were in front of us. As each of them walked through the door, they CHANGED! Eglantine suddenly had heaps and heaps of long golden curls, and as Floreen pushed her out of the way I could see her eyes shining.

Then Floreen was in amongst the sparkles, and OOOOMPH!!! She was wearing the highest high heeled shoes ever, and they were covered with glittering jewels...and she wasn't wobbling even the tiniest bit as she walked!

Perfecta was next. She turned to look at us just before she walked in, and she said in her nastiest voice, "Oh, it's the Rose Roomers! If you're VERY lucky I might wave to you from the Seashell Coach!"

Then she walked into the Great Hall...

...but nothing seemed to happen, except she made a funny kind of 'OH!!!' sound, and sat down hard on the floor.

Alice, Charlotte, Sophia, Emily, Daisy and I were too excited to take much notice. We took a deep breath, and ran into the Great Hall together...

OOOOOOPH!!!

Six GORGEOUS silver ponies were trotting round and round the hall, shaking their silver manes and tails, and whinnying loudly.

They were SO beautiful – but Floreen gave a massive screech, and Lisa screamed. The ponies flung up their heads, and began to gallop.

'Quick!' I said. 'They're scared, poor things! We've got to catch them!'

Which was easier said than done.

Now I know, and I'm sure you do too, that the very worst way to try and catch a pony is to rush around making lots of noise. WE know it – but it looked as if absolutely NONE of my class mates did. Freya whistled at them, Floreen went on screeching, Jemima tried to rush them into a corner...and then Nancy fell off her stilts with a dreadful clatter that sent those POOR ponies into a perfect frenzy. They began to gallop this way and that looking for a way out, but do you know what? Even though they were horribly

frightened they were really careful not to crash into anyone.

They swerved this way and that,
and sometimes they pirouetted on
one silver hoof, and their manes
and tails streamed behind them . . .

"STOP this AT ONCE!"

Queen Gloriana was FURIOUS!
Everyone froze, even the ponies.
The whole Great Hall was as still
and silent as if we'd all been turned
to stone.

"WHO is responsible for this RIDICULOUS state of affairs?" Our head teacher's voice was as cold as ice, and I felt totally terrible. I just wished and WISHED the floor would open and swallow me, but I also knew I had to own up. My knees were like jelly as I croaked, "It was me, Your Majesty."

"Princess Katie, I am DEEPLY disappointed in you," Queen Gloriana snapped, and her eyes were positively flashing. I hung my head. "This is the most SHOCKING—"

But she was interrupted.

Princess Perfecta walked calmly up to our headmistress, sank into a deep curtsey, and spoke in a grown up voice we'd never ever heard her use before.

"If you please, Your Majesty, the fault was not intentional. Our beloved Princess Katie meant no harm. Her wish was for the good of the school, and if Your Majesty will be gracious enough to permit me, I will explain."

Chapter Five

I don't think I've ever been so surprised in my entire life.

Alice grabbed my arm. "It's her WISH!" she said, and her eyes were sparkling. "It's come TRUE!"

Perfecta went on, still in that strange, grown up voice. "Your Majesty must understand that we were each granted one wish.

Princess Katie, having seen the wondrous beauty of the Seashell Coach, was concerned that the piebald ponies were not, perhaps, the most perfect match. With this thought in mind, and in true hopes of doing a good deed, Princess Katie put her own desires to one side, and persuaded her dear friends to follow her noble example...and the result, as you can see, is six delightful silver ponies."

There was a stunned silence, and then everyone began to talk at once. Queen Gloriana held up her hand.

"Thank you, Princess Perfecta," she said. "I accept your explanation. Princess Katie! You and your friends may take your ponies to the royal stable, and..." she actually smiled! 'You may look after them until the Grand Parade tomorrow. The Seashell Coach will be, indeed, quite perfect."

I made my best curtsey ever. "Thank you VERY much, Your Majesty," I said, and we were just moving towards the ponies (they were standing quite still, as good as gold), when Perfecta made a seriously weird noise.

It was a kind of strangled squeak, as if she was trying to stop herself saying something, but absolutely HAD to say it. 'Your Majesty,' she said...or rather, kind of gurgled. "I have one more thing that must be said, for I have a Truthful Heart."

She gulped hard. "Your Majesty, and my fellow princesses, I have to confess to a terrible deed. I knew the importance of our wishes, and I..." she went PUCE, and truly looked as if she was choking on every word "...I stole my wish from the student who won last year.

I am in no way worthy of one hundred tiara points, nor to take my position in the Seashell Coach. I humbly suggest, Your Most Royal Highness, that Princess Katie and her friends take my place."

"Well said, Princess Perfecta," Queen Gloriana said quietly. "It shall be so."

And then Perfecta burst into floods of tears, and rushed out of the Great Hall.

*

We were allowed to look after our ponies for all that afternoon and evening; after all the excitement,

we were excused from lessons. Fairy G said she had to do some private magic on the wooden floor of the great hall, because six feisty little ponies had made a terrible mess, but she didn't sound cross.

She also asked us if we knew that the wishes only lasted for twenty four hours.

"Oh NO!" I said. "Does that mean they'll disappear before the parade?"

Fairy G chuckled. "We might manage an extension," she said. "Just this once. Queen Gloriana thinks you're right, Katie.

The Seashell Coach will look SPLENDID! But they'll have to go after that."

She saw our unhappy faces, and shook her head. "Cheer up! You've each got a hundred tiara points! And think about those poor little piebald ponies, not allowed to take part in the parade. They'll be LONGING for someone to give them a pat, and a piece of apple!"

That made us feel bad. We hurried down to the stables, and they were SO sweet...and, if I'm absolutely truthful, they were even lovelier than our silver ponies because they were so REAL.

Pip

The silver ponies were EXACTLY
the same, so we could never tell
which one was which.

But they did look utterly GORGEOUS the next day, when they came trotting up to collect us for the Royal Parade, and we all stepped into the Seashell Coach.

Chapter Six

So what was the Royal Parade like?

It was HEAVENLY.

Princess Perfecta was still being Truthful of Heart and Full of Grace, and she insisted on doing our hair. She was AMAZING! She even managed to make my hair look princessy.

She clipped it with some little glittery star clips of her own, and it looked WONDERFUL! And then she wished us luck...and you'll never guess what happened next. I found myself actually feeling sorry for her – ME, feeling sorry for Princess Perfecta!

So I asked her if she'd like to ride in the Seashell Coach with us. She gave me a gracious smile, and said in her funny grown-up voice, "You are a true princess, Princess Katie, but I must decline your most generous offer."

So Alice, Emily, Charlotte, Sophia, Daisy and I sat on the white satin cushions with snow-white fur rugs over our knees, and rolled away in the Seashell Coach.

Down the drive we went, and away to the town...and there were THOUSANDS of people cheering and waving at us!

So we smiled, and waved back, and smiled some more until our faces were positively hurting...and when we got back to the Princess Academy we were really tired.

"Phew!" Alice said as we stepped carefully out of the Seashell Coach, trying hard not to step on the hems of our dresses. "That was FUN!"

And then—

OOOMPH!!!

The six silver ponies vanished.

*

So what did we do?

Well...we changed out of our silk and satin and velvet gowns, and then we RAN down to the stables to tell those piebald ponies all about the parade.

And as the littlest pony snuffled her soft whiskery nose into the palm of my hand, hunting for more apple, I felt like the luckiest Princess in the whole wide world. I had a HUNDRED extra tiara points, a pony to pet, and – BEST OF ALL! – six of the very best friends a princess could have. Sophia, Charlotte, Daisy, Emily, Alice – and YOU!

What happens next?
Find out in

and the Dazzling Dragon

Hello! And I SO want to say hello to you properly. Should I say, "Good day Your Majesty?" That doesn't sound very friendly, and I DO want us to be friends! After all, we're at the Princess Academy together, aren't we? Ooops! I nearly forgot to tell you I'm Daisy! Princess Daisy. Have you met my other friends – Charlotte, Katie, Alice, Emily and Sophia? They're learning to be Perfect Princesses, just like you and me. It's fun most of the time, but Princess Perfecta isn't very nice. We're really REALLY happy that she doesn't share the Rose Room dormitory with us.

She's much too horrid!

Check out

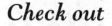

website at:

www.tiaraclub.co.uk

You'll find Perfect Princess games and fun things to do, as well as news on the Tiara Club and all your favourite princesses!

The
Tiara
Club

Win a Tiara Club
Perfect Princess Prize!

Look for the secret word in mirror writing hidden in a tiara in each of the Tiara Club books. Each book has one word. Put together the six words from books 1 to 6 to make a special Perfect Princess sentence, then send it to us. Each month, we will put the correct entries in a draw and one lucky reader will receive a magical Perfect Princess prize!

Send your Perfect Princess sentence, your name and your address on a postcard to:
THE TIARA CLUB COMPETITION,
Orchard Books, 338 Euston Road,
London, NW1 3BH

Australian readers should write to:
Hachette Children's Books,
Level 17/207 Kent Street, Sydney, NSW 2000.

Only one entry per child.
Final draw: 31 October 2006

The Tiara Club

By Vivian French
Illustrated by Sarah Gibb

All priced at £3.99.

The Tiara Club books are available from all good bookshops,
or can be ordered direct from the publisher:
Orchard Books, PO BOX 29, Douglas IM99 1BQ.
Credit card orders please telephone 01624 836000 or fax 01624 837033
or visit our Internet site: www.wattspub.co.uk
or e-mail: bookshop@enterprise.net for details.

To order please quote title, author, ISBN and your full name and address.
Cheques and postal orders should be made payable to 'Bookpost plc.'
Postage and packing is FREE within the UK
(overseas customers should add £2.00 per book).

Prices and availability are subject to change.